Crowd Funding

Crowd Funding

How to Raise Money and Make Money in the Crowd

Modwenna Rees-Mogg

crimson

Crowd Funding: How to Raise Money and Make Money in the Crowd

This first edition published in 2013 by Crimson Publishing Ltd, The Tramshed, Walcot Street, Bath BA1 5BB

© Modwenna Rees-Mogg 2013

The right of Modwenna Rees-Mogg to be identified as the author of this work has been asserted by her in accordance with the Copyright, Designs and Patents Act 1988.

British Library Cataloguing in Publication Data
A catalogue record for this book is available from the British Library

ISBN 978 1 78059 202 2

Typeset by IDSUK (DataConnection) Ltd
Printed and bound in the UK by Bell & Bain Ltd, Glasgow

Contents

Foreword

By Jon Moulton, founder and managing partner of Better Capital

When I started out in venture capital in 1980 it was a niche industry still waiting to be fully formed here in the UK. In the absence of established models of how to invest, the other beginners and I painfully worked out the ways and means necessary to make venture capital work for everyone involved in the market – from the people and institutions who gave us the money to invest, to those who received it. And of course, for ourselves, the fund managers, investing the money and working to get it back at a profit further down the line.

Stepping forward to today, the role of making the crowd funding market succeed has fallen upon the shoulders not just of the owners of the various platforms, but also on the crowd itself – the people, like you, who have already joined the crowd or who will do so soon. You have an unprecedented chance to be a game changer by helping shape the industry through your involvement. And in doing so, you have the opportunity to create wealth for yourself and for others.

There is a lot of money to be made out of crowd funding, which is one of the reasons I have personally invested in Funding Circle, one of the fastest growing platforms today. But whenever there is a lot of money to be made, inevitably there are great risks attached. If you are going to win in a gold rush you need to understand where the money is to be made and how to get your share of it. That is why you need to read books such as this one, which will give you the information you need to get ahead of the masses of other people who also want to win.

When it comes to investing and raising money, crowd funding is, quite simply, the most important development that has happened in a quarter of a century. It is changing the rules completely and is already forcing banks, venture capitalists and others in the market to adapt or die. This is good.

Higher returns will never be risk free but they can be less risky than you think, *if* you act sensibly based on a good level of understanding about what you are doing.

Entrepreneurs can create exciting new business models where anyone from friends to potential customers – and even complete strangers – can become your funders and engage with you in an ongoing dialogue from the day you start your business. This 360 degree engagement brings with it an inevitable improvement in how businesses are run and how they grow. And the better everyone gets at crowd funding, the cheaper and quicker it will become.

I cannot think of any reason why most adults should not take a look at crowd funding. Indeed, most of you will have already done so by using donation-based sites such as www.justgiving.com, but before you do anything potentially expensive in the crowd I recommend you do your research. That is why you need to read this book. Now.

April 2013

Introduction

Welcome crowd funders: here is your book

Crowd funding. What a brilliant term. It does just what it says on the tin. Or does it? By the end of this book I hope you (and I) will be able to answer that question with a lot more certainty than now.

As one of the most explosive developments on the internet in the last two to three years, the time is now right to take a good look at crowd funding.

Normally, a book of this type would be driven by the author (me) doing lots of research, analysing what is uncovered, and then writing it up and commenting upon it. But the very nature of crowd funding encouraged me to take a different approach. When it comes to crowd funding, the people best positioned to explain all about it are those involved in it. So I have built this book on that basis. With the support of many crowd funding platform operators, entrepreneurs and investors, and with tactical use of the web to reach out to others, my team and I have gathered and sieved the facts, stories and anecdotes and put them into a format that makes it as relevant and interesting as possible to you, the reader. This book is packed full of useful and fascinating case studies and comments from entrepreneurs and investors active in crowd funding today. The stories of these trailblazers will prove to you that you, too, can make a great success of any crowd funding campaign.

The result of all the research and work is that this book is a full guide to crowd funding and to all the different types on offer today, ranging from how to ensure your fundraising succeeds to how to put your donation or investment to best use. It includes everything from a history of crowd funding to a vision for the future, and even how to set up your own crowd funding platform.

Some of the highlights inside are listed below.

The different types of crowd funding

- **Donation:** when funders simply donate money to the fundraiser.
- **Pledge:** when funders "pre-order" goods (from music and films to consumer goods and more), paying the cash upfront to the business so they have the money needed to make the goods.
- **Debt:** when funders lend money to fundraisers and receive interest and the capital back over time.
- **Alternative debt:** when funders lend money to fundraisers secured on real assets such as invoices or property.
- **Equity:** when funders buy shares (equity) in a company in return for cash.
- **Social enterprise:** when funders buy, lend or invest, but with an angle that does social good as well as giving the funder a reward or return.
- **Specialist platforms:** when funders are offered only very specific opportunities that comply with the rules of the specialist platform, e.g. only app development projects or sharia-compliant fundraisings.
- **Multiple platforms:** when fundraisers are given the opportunity to fundraise via all the different types of fundraising.

How to benefit from a crowd funding opportunity

Fundraisers

I will help you to understand which platforms are right for you and why. You will learn how to create a campaign, including lots of stuff on planning and organisation so that you optimise the chances of success. You will learn about the different types of funders, what they like and don't like, and how to ensure that you attract the right ones to your campaign. And inside are the answers to the challenging questions your funders may ask you, as well as tips on how to look after them once they have funded you.

Investors

For funders and investors, this book is essential reading. Crowd funding is exciting but it is also risky. You will learn all about the different types of crowd funding and which ones are suitable for you. It will tell you what to look out for in a campaign before you invest your money and it will explain what you should expect during and after a campaign.

People wanting to build a crowd funding platform or business on the back of the crowd

This is the first book, I believe, that explains what you need to do to set up your own crowd funding platform. It includes all the things you need to think about, from practical stuff to all the things that entrepreneurs often forget, such as getting the right insurance in place. I have also explained how professional advisers and other businesses can earn from getting involved in crowd funding.

All the extra stuff that other books have ignored

With some trepidation, but with a greater desire to be interesting than to be right, I have included some ideas on how I think crowd funding might develop in the short to medium term. I have also sought out expert contributors to add appendices on legal issues, the UK tax break schemes that make crowd equity investing so attractive to investors, and a glossary of terms that you will come across in the crowd. Last but not least, for those interested in how the phenomenon that is crowd funding came about, there is also a useful history that sets the whole opportunity in context.

I hope, if you are not yet hanging out in the crowd, that by the end of this book you will have joined us. And I will keep my fingers crossed that when you do come on board, after reading this handbook, you will be as well prepared as possible to enjoy the ride.

So a warm welcome to the crowd.

Why this book?

Crowd funding has been around for a long time. Jenny McLaren, who worked as my researcher and assistant on this book, has written a short history which is well worth reading (see Appendix II). There are some lovely stories from the past about how crowds have funded projects – check out the case study below, told to me by David Wragg of Saffery Champness when he heard I was writing this book, on how the money for the pedestal of the Statue of Liberty was raised.

Case study

One of the first crowd fundings ever?

I believe that crowd funding as we understand it today was actually devised in the late 19th century because of this story.

It is generally widely known that France gave the Statue of Liberty to the United States as a gift, in 1886. It is not so commonly known that the US had to fund the pedestal upon which the statute stands. The pedestal cost $334,000 and when the fundraising committee began to run out of time, they approached Joseph Pulitzer, the newspaper owner to assist them.

Joseph Pulitzer launched a campaign to invite the citizens of New York to donate even small amounts to help in the funding of the pedestal. Donors were offered miniature replicas of the statue in return. The 19th-century crowd funding campaign raised approximately $100,000 and gave the fundraising a welcome boost.

I have spent the last 12 years largely occupied with building my business and expertise in the business angel world (see page 28), one of the most fascinating and, in my view, important parts of the financial services market. Until relatively recently I have largely been an observer of the "crowd funders". Over the last 18 months, however, this "cousin" of the angel world has turned from a tadpole into a Goliath frog – in the US, in the UK, and it seems in just about every other major economy in the world. That growth has taken place in less than four years in the US, and less than three in the UK.

My first exposure to crowd funding was a couple of years ago, when I heard on the grapevine that an entrepreneur of great talent, whom I vaguely knew, was planning on solving his company's particular funding gap by doing a crowd investment. The next thing I heard was that this person, Charles Armstrong, founder of Trampoline Systems, had been successful. It was a small, isolated incident, or so I thought at the time.

Case study

Trampoline Systems

In 2009, Trampoline Systems, the award-winning enterprise software vendor, was one of the first businesses to raise money through equity crowd funding. The company announced its plan to raise £1m through four rounds of funding. The first round was completed in October 2009 and raised £260,000, with a second round of £350,000 opening in August 2010. Trampoline worked closely with legal advisers to ensure that its crowd funding process complied with the then Financial Services Authority (FSA) regulations. The company invited expressions of interest only from people certified as high net worth individuals or as sophisticated investors, plus Trampoline's existing shareholders.

The London-based company's SONAR CRM product helps customers increase the win rate in business-to-business (B2B) sales. They decided to use crowd funding as a method when the total amount invested by venture capitalists dropped by 36% in 2009. They saw the chance to use crowd funding in a different way, and worked with the FSA to work out how they could raise finance in exchange for equity. They believe that crowd funding could be the future for small businesses and that it gives entrepreneurs an alternative source of funding.

Back in 2010, I was sitting in my office one evening just before Christmas. I took a call from an entrepreneur who wanted to buy one of the investment adverts we circulated to the investors who subscribe to AngelNews. I tried to refuse to sell him one – "Better off buying it after the holidays when the investors are back," I told him – but he bluntly told me that he did not want it so he could access our investors. He wanted it because it would be a legitimate way in which he could tell his base of thousands of enthusiasts for his cool bike about his fundraising need. I sold him the advert. Two days later I was staggered to hear that he had already had commitments of over £1m from his "crowd".

All went quiet for me on crowd funding until 2011, although there was quite a lot of talk about the new online peer-to-peer lending businesses such as Zopa getting going. For me, 2011 was the year crowd funding started to take hold in the UK. In the spring, a man called Anil Stocker called me – he had been told to introduce himself to me so he could explain about the start-up he had founded with friend Charlie Delingpole, MarketInvoice. We met. Half a cup of coffee later I was hooked. MarketInvoice, which auctions invoices to private investors ranging from individuals to Family Offices (private companies who manage the finances of a single wealthy family), is one of those sweet businesses where everyone wins. Businesses get their money quicker and at a better price than otherwise, investors make a great return for the risk they are taking, and the platform operator does profitable business getting the two together.

Within weeks another couple of men had also offered me a cup of coffee to introduce themselves. They were Darren Westlake and Luke Lang, the founders of Crowdcube. (By the way, in Appendix III you will find details for MarketInvoice, Crowdcube and their ilk.) Another coffee and I now knew about another genius business model that had uncovered a legally valid alternative route for entrepreneurs to raise investment rather than through the banks, business angels or venture capitalists.

Since then my relationship with crowd funding has become more and more exciting – sometimes it seems that everyone is at it. My old friend Kevin Caley has set up ThinCats, which provides debt funding by the crowd for small and medium-sized enterprises (SMEs); Jon Moulton and many others have backed Funding Circle; there's Platform Black, which is also in the invoice auction space; Seedrs, which is doing equity crowd funding; and Karen Darby has just set up CrowdMission to raise investment for social enterprises. There's Rebuilding Society, Bank to the Future, Trillion Fund, Abundance Generation and many more appearing all the time. And now Kickstarter, the granddaddy of crowd funding, has opened for business in the UK. Even the UK government is now on board, providing millions of pounds in cash to the debt crowd funding platforms and working closely with platform operators to create suitable regulatory frameworks that will enable the markets to work effectively while protecting those who use them.

Exciting times indeed. Like it or not, everyone involved in enterprise and, therefore inevitably, early stage funding is now on this journey. Not everyone will engage with it, but you ignore it at your peril.

In the future I am certain crowd funding will move further. There will be more and more stories, some of which will be even bigger, more colourful or perhaps more scandalous than those I have included. I am certain the rules and regulations surrounding crowd funding will also move on, and there is no doubt whatsoever that there will be far more innovation in this market before it finally matures. But some things will remain true throughout time: things such as how to make a successful pitch or, if you are an investor, how to tell a great opportunity from a poor one. Ensuring that a light is shone on these truths is the underlying purpose of this book, and its success will be judged on whether you, the crowd, decide that it does the job you need it to.

Part One

What is crowd funding?

Chapter 1

Not all crowds or fundraisings are the same

Crowd funding is an umbrella term for a wide variety of types of fundraising undertaken by individuals and businesses, but essentially all types of crowd funding are the same in that an individual or a business reaches out to the crowd to obtain money in order to achieve an objective. This ranges from funding a creative project to a full equity fundraising for an established company.

There are dozens of different ways fundraisers and donors/investors "do" crowd funding, but the common thread is that many individuals come together to donate or invest as little as £10 each to help fund the need. With enough investors, the fundraising can be completed. Don't imagine, though, that crowd funding is just for the £10 punter. On some sites, especially the crowd equity ones, it is possible to invest tens of thousands of pounds if you wish – either in just one business or spread across many. And don't think that using the funding is a free meal ticket to your funding needs. You pay fees to fundraise from the crowd, which are taken out of the funds raised. Remember that the relationship between fundraiser and donor/investor typically lasts long after the fundraising campaign is complete.

The first thing you need to understand is that there are eight main crowd funding subsets, which are explained below – within those there are many more.

The main types of crowd funding

Donation funding

Arguably the latest evolution in crowd funding started with the rise of donation funding sites. Here in the UK almost everyone will have heard of, if not have donated to charity via, www.justgiving.com and www. virginmoneygiving.com. Typically, individuals undertaking a charity fundraising, e.g. running a marathon, use these sites to collect donations from their friends. The charity sites enable donations to be made but also have the advantage of letting charities get extra money from the Gift Aid scheme, whereby UK taxpayers can allow the charity to reclaim tax on the donation.

As well as charity sites, there are other sites that allow you to raise money for non-commercial objectives, such as www.gofundme.com and www.gogetfunding.com. These sites are used for everything from helping an individual to raise money to go travelling, to providing funding to pay for unforeseen medical expenses or other expensive crisis situations that the person needing money cannot afford to pay for themselves.

As with other types of crowd funding sites, donors can give money in tiny amounts, including just a few pounds. Fees are usually less than 5% and sometimes have a minimum cost per donation made.

The most well known donation platforms are:

- **US:** www.gofundme.com, www.rockethub.com, http://peerbackers.com, www.sponsume.com, www.causes.com, www.crowdrise.com, www.fundageek.com
- **UK:** www.justgiving.com, www.virginmoneygiving.com
- **Elsewhere:** www.babyloan.org/en (France, but also international), www.pozible.com (Australia).

Case study

Help Farrah

GoFundMe is a slightly different crowd funding site, as it not only allows people to raise money for their creative projects and businesses, but also for personal reasons such as holidays, religions and fulfilling their dreams. As a donation-based site, it allows, for example, people to help fund someone's education. On 20th July 2012, Victoria Albright started a campaign for Farrah Soudani, who was one of the people injured in the mass shooting in a movie theatre in Aurora, Colorado during a midnight screening of The Dark Knight Rises. *Victoria says that Farrah was hit by an explosive that took out much of her mid-section and left leg. While being treated at an intensive care unit, Farrah did not have medical insurance and her mother is taking time off work to care for her daughter. The campaign was to help pay the medical bills and to ensure that Farrah's family can survive while her mother is out of work. At the time of the page closing in December 2012, Farrah had moved home with her mother and the money raised was helping with ongoing doctors' bills and helping her to regain her independence. In total, they raised $171,525 to help her get back on her feet.*

Pledge or project funding

Crowd funding originated with pledge funding for projects. Long before the arrival of Kickstarter, IndieGoGo and their like, people who had no money available to get a project going would pre-sell their products to generate the money they needed to make them and get them to their customers. Typically, though, these were localised affairs and quite sporadic. And for many years all charities worth their salt would fundraise from the general public, taking donations from everyone from strangers (often via a collecting tin in the street) to their closest supporters.

The big difference with a crowd funded project is the scale and the degree of sophistication which has evolved thanks to the internet. Online crowd funding for projects has created an open playing field – you can fundraise from just about anyone. The popularity of crowd funding in the indie film world is possibly a sign of what is to come: 10%

of films at Sundance last year were at least partly funded by Kickstarter campaigns.

Pledge funding is unique in that you are raising money to fund a specific project. The transaction is simple. You fundraise and promise to deliver the product (e.g. a film) or service (e.g. a concert) in return for a pledge payment in advance. Once you have delivered, the contract is completed. The donor has no legal right to get involved in how you create or deliver your service, but if you fail to deliver it you have breached your contract with them.

Crowd funded projects are never this simple, though. Thanks to the transparency of online sites and the innate competitiveness of crowd funders, a typical crowd funded project is much more sophisticated than a one-stop "ask".

For a start, you can crowd fund a project with just a few words on a web page or by sending out an email to your friends, but this is unlikely to be successful as competition for money is fierce. If you fundraise via a crowd funding platform, you need to make your case for why you want the money in the best way that you can. You need a video, persuasive wording and a sophisticated offer to gain the attention and support of the crowd.

The big change from traditional types of fundraising, such as looking for angel or venture capital or debt finance, is that with crowd funding you can offer different levels of rewards for different sizes of pledge. For example, if this book had not been commissioned in the normal way by Crimson Publishing, I might have decided to crowd fund it via a site such as Kickstarter, or even approached the dedicated crowd funding publisher Unbound (http://unbound.co.uk). I might have asked for a small donation of £10 now and promised to send you a copy of the book once it was published. For £20 I could have promised you a signed copy. For £100 I might have promised you a copy, but also promised to come and talk to you personally about what I know about crowd funding. I would have asked for as many £10 pledges as possible, as I know that I could profitably deliver as many copies of the book as I had orders at this price. However, in order to make the signed copies more valuable, I might have limited the signed copies to 100 only. And I might have wanted to talk personally to only 10 people, so would only allow 10 people to "donate" at the £100 level.

Later on in the book we will go into all this in more detail.

Case study

Pebble e-paper watch

Probably one of the most famous successes of crowd funding is the Pebble smart watch that launched the company's fundraising campaign on Kickstarter in April 2011. Pebble set the initial target at $100,000, which would be raised through donations and by people pre-ordering the watch. For $115 you could get a black Pebble watch, or you could order it in another colour for $125. For donations over $235, they offered a "Hacker special" that allowed people to start writing their own coding for the watch before other people even received theirs. Larger donations got you multiple watches and the chance to customise your watch face. Rumour has it that when "the crowd" saw that the fundraising was going well, there was a viral enthusiasm among donors to see if they could get the fundraising to over $10m – and they did! In just 38 days, Pebble had received pledges from nearly 69,000 people totalling over $10m. While this seems like a runaway success on the face of it, the company had not anticipated such interest, and therefore it has faced major challenges with suddenly having a much bigger business than anticipated. They had to completely rethink the business, scaling it up to meet the demand. However, with the money raised, they have been able to achieve this; they have begun mass production and are now shipping product. In fact it is a "must have" gadget for many cool investors and entrepreneurs.

The most well known pledge platforms are:

- **US:** www.kickstarter.com (now also open in the UK), www.indiegogo.com, www.gofundme.com, www.rockethub.com, http://peerbackers.com, www.sellaband.com, www.quirky.com, www.crowtilt.com
- **UK:** www.crowdfunder.co.uk, www.wefund.com

- **Elsewhere:** www.indulj.be (Hungary), www.pozible.com (Australia, spreading globally), www.lanzanos.com (Spain), www.fondomat.com (Czech Republic), www.fundrazr.com (Canada), www.headstart.co.il (Israel).

Straight debt funding

Crowd lending is more often known as peer to-peer lending. Essentially, rather than using banks, if companies or individuals want to borrow money, they apply for the funds they want via the online website. Investors on the site then join together to lend the funds. The borrower does not usually know who is lending to them and repays the loan to the platform, which then returns the interest and the capital to the lenders, taking a fee on the way through.

By no means do all people or businesses who apply for a loan get accepted by the operators of these sites. Typically, 85% of applicants will be rejected because the site operator does not deem them credit worthy; the rejection rate can be as high as 99%. Crowd lending sites will expect you to provide lots of financial information, and they will perform credit checks, review business plans and do pretty much everything else a normal bank would do. The difference is that instead of going to a credit committee in an anonymous building somewhere in a bank where they will decide whether to lend to you, the loan request is posted online and investors are invited to offer the funds to lend.

Case study

The Cashmere Centre

The Cashmere Centre is a Buckinghamshire-based mail order provider of high-quality cashmere and currently offers the largest range by mail order in the UK. However, to meet stock requirements during peak periods, such as Christmas, it required funding to continue to meet this demand, as well as to improve the functionality of its website for customers. It used Funding Circle, an online marketplace designed to help businesses find fast finance and to help investors get better returns. After just 14 days the company had borrowed funds of over £40,000 from more than 507 investors to build up its e-commerce system. With the process being cheaper, quicker and easier than going through the high street banks, The Cashmere Centre was able to concentrate on growing its business with no restrictions.

The most well known debt funding platforms are:

- **US:** www.somolend.com, www.lendingclub.com, www.prosper.com
- **UK:** www.fundingcircle.com, www.zopa.com, www.thincats.com, www.ratesetter.com
- **Elsewhere:** www.booomerang.dk (Denmark).

Specialist debt funding

Crowd lending has rapidly become very varied. There is now a number of sites that do alternative types of lending such as asset-based lending (i.e. lending against the physical assets a business owns) as well as sites that lend against a business's debtor book (i.e. against outstanding invoices owed to the business). Essentially, these are ways of lending that are less risky for the lender because there is a real asset in place that supports the loan and can be called upon (i.e. taken on and then sold by the lender) if the loan is not repaid.

One interesting recent site is www.crowdahouse.com, which helps investors build a portfolio of buy-to-let properties in the UK.

Case study

Ingenium

In 2010, Dan Collier and James Murphy brought together over 30 years of experience to create ITS Ingenium, a next generation talent management and integrated IT recruitment consultancy, focused on areas such as financial services, investment banking and capital markets, asset and investment management, hedge funds, e-commerce and social media. With an eight-month turnover of £300,000, they were looking to scale rapidly and to do more work in the contract market, which required a flexible source of funding. Ingenium was paying contract IT workers after 14 days to attract the best talent, but typically the end customers would pay Ingenium after 30–45 days. Despite their strong contacts and networks, the founders' one-year track record limited their funding options. With their bank promoting a factoring solution that involved outsourcing credit control (and potentially damaging their reputation with key customers), and high monthly service fees regardless of whether they drew down funding or not, the founders turned to MarketInvoice. Their flexibility allowed Ingenium to keep its good relationships with its clients while receiving the funding on the invoices at a low rate.

The most well known specialist debt funding platforms are:

- **US:** www.receivablesexchange.com
- **UK:** www.marketinvoice.com, www.platformblack.com, www.crowdahouse.com.

Equity funding

In an equity fundraising, businesses sell shares in their business to the crowd in return for cash. They may offer special rewards as well as an incentive to the investors. The investors become shareholders in the company with all the legal rights that this entails, for example the right to dividends and the right to sell their shares to other people one day.

This is the area of crowd funding that has caused the most controversy of all. In fact, in the US it has been so controversial and yet so successful that the US government has been forced to change securities law via the JOBS Act (Jumpstart Our Business Startups) to accommodate this type of fundraising. In the UK there is still a lot of controversy surrounding equity crowd funding and which individuals may be approached to invest. One of the main principles of investment regulation in recent years has been to protect the small investor from making risky investments where they can lose their money. However, this has come into conflict with equity crowd funding, the specific purpose of which is to allow investors to make as many small investments into companies as they wish, perhaps very small sums of money per investment, and to allow friends, family and even strangers to invest in a business that they think has exciting prospects and will give them a return on their investment. I know a great regulatory expert called Gillian Roche-Saunders and she has very helpfully written about this issue in Appendix V.

One interesting adaptation of the equity crowd funding model is www. sprowd.com, where donors do not become shareholders in a fundraising business but do get hard cash returned to them by the fundraiser in due course.

Case study

Kammerlings

Kammerlings ginseng spirit began life in Highbury, North London, with ex-bartender and self-confessed drinks geek Alex Kammerling. He was inspired by the history of alcoholic drinks being infused with natural botanicals as a medicine (in theory, the alcohol preserves the active ingredients from the botanicals and delivers them effectively into the bloodstream). He wanted to create a unique, versatile and tasty spirit that had a lower alcohol content than the regular 40% alcohol by volume (abv). This led him to create Kamm & Sons – a drink that is made in a similar way to gin but contains 45 natural botanicals including ginseng, fresh grapefruit peel and manuka honey, with a lighter 33% abv. Kammerling needed funding to increase both his production and sales in the UK market so that he could distribute his products to high-end stores such as Selfridges and Harvey Nichols. He aimed to launch in select bars overseas with the goal of making the brand global. To raise funding, he turned to Crowdcube. Kammerlings offered 23% equity for £180,000 – a target that was reached in three months with the help of 85 investors.

Nearly two years after it secured its first round of funding, Kammerlings raised a further £325,000 in February 2013 from 64 investors in return for 28.6% of the business, again through Crowdcube. Kammerlings intends to use this second round of funding to export to the more discerning and health conscious drinkers in Europe, Asia and America, as well as to high-growth markets such as China. The company is currently exporting to Sweden, France and Spain.

Since it launched in April 2011 Kamm & Sons (trading as Kammerlings Ltd) has sold more than 5,000 bottles. It is available in prestigious five-star hotels, restaurants and cocktail bars and through wholesalers throughout the UK.

With over 17 years of experience in the drinks industry, Alex has kept the recipe a closely guarded secret between him and a few family members. After the second round of funding, Alex said: "Crowd funding is proving that businesses like ours can raise the money they need to grow not just in the UK but also abroad. We want to sell more than 15,000 units this year and this investment will help us to achieve that growth target. We didn't even consider the banks for this round because the 17% APR interest rates are too high for a small business like ours."

The most well known crowd equity platforms are:

- **US:** www.growvc.com (also in Europe), Angellist www.angel.co, www.seedups.com, www.secondmarket.com, www.earlyshares.com, www.fundable.com, www.startupvalley.com
- **UK:** www.crowdcube.com, www.seedeisplatform.com, www.justinvesting.com, www.syndicateroom.com
- **Elsewhere:** http://eureeca.com (global, but founded by Brits), www.companisto.de (Germany), www.innovestment.de (Germany), www.venturebonsai.com (Finland), www.fundedbyme.com (Finland and Sweden), www.sprowd.com (Netherlands), www.gambitious.com (Netherlands), www.moneycrowd.org (Ireland), www.symbid.com (Netherlands).

Social enterprise funding

As the crowd funding opportunity has expanded so has the variety of sites offering crowd funding solutions. The latest subset that appears to be gaining traction is the area of social enterprise funding: this covers the spectrum from charity to for-profit business where the underlying activity has a defined social purpose. Social enterprise funding should not, by the way, be confused with social media, which is basically doing marketing and PR via the web, email and social networks. The social purpose may be something as simple as employing people who have previously been unemployed in a mainstream business or as complicated as a biotech company wanting to create a new drug to eradicate malaria.

Social funding is different in that one of the main rewards for donors is the satisfaction of doing something good in the world. I Increasingly, however, the lines between the "not-for-profit" or charity world and straightforward commerce are blurring. If anything, crowd funding will hasten a further collapse of these lines as businesses see the benefits to their brand and corporate culture of doing something good while making a profit and traditional not-for-profit attitudes become more commercial in order to create a strong financial underpinning that makes them sustainable in the long term.

Within the social enterprise funding arena are sites that enable microfinance projects to get funded, where donors give money to a worthwhile project but the recipient agrees to repay the money over time. These types of site have proved very popular with western donors looking to find ways to help entrepreneurial individuals in the third world, so that they can build a microbusiness that will lift them and their friends and relations out of poverty. Great examples are www.kiva. org and www.babyloan.org/en.

Case study

Flaura Ingabire

At the age of just eight, Flaura fled into the bush with her brother and sister to hide from the genocidaires attacking her village of Byumba, Rwanda. With her father killed and her mother left with injuries so debilitating she had regular hospital visits and was unable to work, Flaura didn't have the easiest start in life. However, she started her first business at just 16 years old, opening a bar in her village during her

> school holidays. Now 22 years old, she has sold the bar and is running a canteen at her university, and she used a loan through Kiva to buy a photocopier. At her university, the professors do not have enough copies of the handouts, so by purchasing a photocopier she is allowing all students access to course material, as well as earning herself $40 a week profit. This, combined with the profits from her canteen, allows her to pay her university fees, her brother's and sister's school fees and for her mother's trips to hospital. Flaura is hoping to take out a second Kiva loan later this year to expand her canteen into a fully fledged cafeteria – her university has nowhere to buy food – and to install some computers with internet access, as there are none at her university. Flaura initially used her work and loans to support her family, but she is now expanding to help her fellow students.

The most well known social funding platforms are:

- **US:** www.kiva.org, www.razoo.com, www.startsomegood.com, www.wahooly.com, www.40billion.com
- **UK:** www.rebuildingsociety.com, www.buzzbnk.org, www.crowdmission.com
- **Elsewhere:** www.babyloan.org/en (France).

Specialist crowd platforms

We are already seeing a rise in specialist crowd platforms that are focused on a particular sector or stage. One of the most buzzy sectors for investment in recent years has been clean tech and green tech, so it is no surprise that there is now a crowd platform (www.abundancegeneration.com) that focuses on just clean tech and green tech projects and investment opportunities.

In an interesting development, a sharia-compliant platform has just launched called www.shekra.com, which blends Islamic finance principles with crowd funding.

The most buzzy area of all is in creative projects. There are dozens of sites specialising in this field, many of which are highly focused;

examples include www.appbackr.com and www.appsfunder.com, which allow app developers to raise money easily. There are also sites focused on music and other creative arts, such as www.pledgemusic.com and www.ulule.com. Typically on these sites, fundraisers can raise as little as $500 and the maximum amount they can raise is usually capped, for example at $100,000.

Another area of specialisation is in medical research and development. Sites such as www.medstartr.com, www.petridish.org and www.rally.org focus on this area. And for those who have challenges funding their education, there are sites such as www.crowdfundedu.com, and www.funding4learning.com.

Case study

braGGs

braGGs came about after a group of women were struggling to find correct bras for themselves after their mastectomies and reconstructive surgeries. When they decided to have a breast reconstruction, they were opting not to have to wear prostheses. However, they found that to get a natural-shaped breast (and avoid large indentations at the front of their bras), they had to wear a mastectomy bra with a full prosthesis over the implant; so they decided to make a better solution. They were motivated to create a bra for the reconstructed girl! After looking at the problems women face after having reconstructive surgery, they designed the bras to solve the issue of gaps and to provide additional support for the implants, and they used stretchy fabric to fit every woman's unique shape. A braGGs bra is not a mastectomy bra or a regular bra; braGGs bras are reconstruction bras. They aimed to raise $10,000 on MedStartr – a website specifically for medical start-ups and healthcare innovations – and reached that goal with the help of just 51 backers. With shockingly high statistics of more than 200,000 women diagnosed with breast cancer and approximately 97,000 breast reconstruction procedures each year in the United States alone, they knew that there was demand for a product like theirs for fellow survivors of breast cancer.

In the US, www.circleup.com is designed to help with fundraising for established companies in sectors that are less attractive to the venture capital market because they are unlikely to show the explosive growth potential of a typical high-tech internet business. It allows companies with $1m–$10m in revenue to fundraise on its platform and has restricted its sector focus to food, agriculture, retail and other consumer-oriented businesses. Interestingly, fast-moving consumer goods (FMCG) giant Procter & Gamble has formed a partnership with CircleUp to help support the creation of new businesses in the FMCG space.

One great advantage crowd funding has for companies in these sectors is that the crowd that is funding them is also likely to be the consumers of the products they are selling, so there is an intrinsic alignment of interest for funders.

There is also now a site for crowd funding for scientific research called www.microryza.com, which is very altruistic. All the scientists and researchers keep 100% ownership of the research and the results they gather as a result of the funding they receive.

Case study

Wormfree World

Wormfree World set up a crowd funding campaign on Microryza to help raise money for their efforts to help the 400,000,000 children in the world who suffer from worms. Microryza is a site designed specifically for research projects to allow funders to get involved with projects all around the world. Wormfree World's three-fold mission for their research institute is, firstly, to discover and develop urgently needed cures; secondly, to create simple and robust diagnostics; and finally, to engage and educate to bring awareness, treatment and prevention. They hoped to raise $15,000 to enable their scientist to perform 1,000 screens over the following three months, and to purchase worms and essential research supplies such as plates, solutions, tubes and gloves. They exceeded their target and reached nearly $19,000 to help with their research, which kicked off in December 2012 with the first stage of the plan – sorting the compounds ready for analysis.

These sites are no different from other sites except for the fact that they focus on a sector or stage of company development, or are more restricted as to which investors can sign up or the sums they are allowed to invest.

Multiple funding platforms

While most platforms choose to specialise in specific types of fundraising, there are others that are taking a different approach – offering their fundraisers the opportunity to use one platform to raise many different types of finance. The launch of https://banktothefuture. com in the UK at the end of 2012 is a very interesting example of this. At BankToTheFuture.com, the founder, Simon Dixon, has created a site where investors can invest for shares (equity) and/or for debt and also do charity fundraising all on the same platform.

Case study

Peace One Day

The Peace One Day campaign was one of the first successful fundraisings on BankToTheFuture.com. It just succeeded in exceeding its goal of £7,000 to make Peace One Day a globally institutionalised day – putting it on a par with Mother's Day and Father's Day. Peace One Day falls on 21st September and is a day to celebrate peace and a global ceasefire. The founders believe the impact of this day is more than just a symbolic gesture; it also provides UN agencies and humanitarian organisations with the chance to focus their lifesaving work and plan for this day. The founders raised £7,089 against a maximum target of £10,000, but because they exceeded their minimum target of £7,000 they were able to keep the money because the campaign was on behalf of a charity. Donors received a thank-you on the website for £10, and for £50 they also received a T-shirt. If anyone had made a top donation of £25,000 or more, they would have been given VIP tickets to concerts, access to boardroom meetings and an annual dinner with the patrons of the charity.

How the traditional investment market is reacting to the arrival of crowd funding

Although I am convinced that crowd funding in its various guises is here to stay, you should not be misled into thinking that the traditional routes to getting money to fund your business are going to disappear. Investors and the people who advise entrepreneurs and investors are intelligent people. It is no surprise, therefore, that they are already reacting to the competitive threat from crowd funding by rethinking their approach to how they make themselves attractive to businesses looking for money and to the investors who want to back them.

Before the arrival of crowd funding, if you wanted to raise finance for your business or project you typically had three choices: bank lending, venture capital or business angels.

Bank lending

While it is easy to find a bank, many banks were (and continue to be) unwilling to lend the sums of money many businesses need to grow really quickly, especially when those businesses are at an early stage of development. The reason that banks are often reluctant to lend is that the risks to them if you don't pay back the loan are high. One failed loan can wipe out the profits they have made on successful loans to other businesses. Banks therefore like to assure themselves as far as possible that loans will be repaid. They typically do this by examining the borrowing request in minute detail and by asking for other forms of security, such as the right to take charge over another asset owned by the borrower (or the directors of the company if the borrower is a company) and personal guarantees from the directors and/or shareholders of the company that they will repay the loan personally if the borrower cannot do so. The effect for the borrower is that if they cannot repay the loan, the bank will take ownership of the asset they have charged and sell it to get their money back, or they may insist that the guarantor personally pays the money owed. Banks are differentiating themselves by offering customers a private way of borrowing, and in the UK they are learning to speed up the time it takes to process loans. For example, at the time of writing Barclays is claiming to have reduced the process time from several months to six weeks. It would not surprise me, though, if we see one or more banks building a quasi-crowd fund offer soon.

Venture capital

Venture capitalists were, and still are, relatively easy to find. They have websites and their trade associations have directories of fund managers you can approach, either directly or (a better option) through advisers such as corporate financiers or lawyers. In the UK, the trade association for venture capitalists is called the British Private Equity and Venture Capital Association (www.bvca.co.uk).

Interestingly, some of the largest and most successful venture capitalists are investing in crowd funding platforms; for example, Index Ventures and Union Square Ventures have backed Funding Circle (www.fundingcircle. com). There are also some venture capitalists who already help private investors invest in entrepreneurs. In the UK, some venture capitalists raise money from private individuals by selling them shares in quoted companies known as venture capital trusts. They use the funds they raise to invest directly in high-growth-potential businesses. The UK government supports these venture capitalists by giving investors income tax breaks on the new shares they buy in the venture capital trust, and also by allowing the dividends the venture capital trust pays to be tax – free. For investors, another attraction is that they can sell the shares in a venture capital trust via their stockbroker. Be warned though – you have to hold the shares for five years before you sell if you want to keep the tax breaks the government offers.

Another way in which venture capitalists help private investors back companies is via the UK government's Enterprise Investment Scheme (EIS). Fund managers such as Calculus Capital, Mercia, MMC Ventures, Octopus Ventures and Oxford Capital Partners raise EIS funds, whereby they raise money from private investors (with lots of tax breaks attached) and pool it to invest in companies. You can find out a lot more information on the EIS in Appendix VI. One of the chief reasons investors invest in venture capital trusts and EIS funds is that they can invest passively and rely on the fund manager to work for them to manage the investments and help grow them so they sell at a large profit.

Business angels

The business angel market is reacting to crowd funding in an interesting way. Before the arrival of crowd funding, to find business angels you had either to informally reach them through your own contacts or to approach them via a business angel network. Over the last decades of the 20th century a cottage industry developed around business angels; a person or a small team of people would create a business that specialised in gathering together groups of angel investors and then in showing them businesses that needed funding. These groups became known as business angel networks or clubs. Loads of different models for these networks developed, from the highly secretive – you can only find us by personal recommendation – through to very public networks such as Venture Capital Report, where I worked in the early Noughties.

In the past, business angel networks tended to work as middlemen between the entrepreneur and the investor, sometimes charging fees to both investors and entrepreneurs and sometimes just charging one side. The levels of advice they provided varied widely, from offering pretty much none at all to giving lots of support to the entrepreneur on getting "investor ready". Investors and entrepreneurs were introduced to each other via the network, usually at a live meeting where the entrepreneur "pitched" their idea to a room full of investors, but the matching of the perfect investor to the ideal company was pretty random. For around one or two in 10 it worked, but for the rest it was just a case of bad luck and try again sometime. Most networks could help a company raise maybe a few hundred thousand pounds, but often the sums were smaller than that. This meant that an entrepreneur would have to use many networks to get all the money they needed and would have to take responsibility for gathering all the random investors and processing and closing the fundraising round. This is no mean feat for a typical entrepreneur, who is already madly busy trying to get their business up and running and who may never have fundraised before. With the upsurge in use of the internet, a number of networks have now raised their profile online, creating websites where you could see profiles of companies that were fundraising and sending out emails with those profiles to investors to encourage them to come forward and look at the deal on offer. The networks typically made money by charging fees from entrepreneurs and/or investors including "pay to pitch", success commissions, monthly retainers and membership fees (the latter from the investors). Many networks still operate in this way; the most well known include www. beerandpartners.com, www.xenos.co.uk, www.lbangels.co.uk, www.yaba. org.uk, www.swain.org.uk and www.envestors.co.uk.

Case study

eReceipts

eReceipts is an electronic solution to the problem of managing, storing and retrieving receipts. eReceipts are created and collected from retailers' point of sale systems and held in the cloud for access by consumers through their mobile or web devices. PRL – the company behind eReceipts – had already signed up over 110 independent retailers, and arranged for the system to be deployed in one of the UK's leading supermarkets, before it started its fundraising. To help them sign up more retailers and to continue growing, the company undertook a second fundraising round of £1m. For a portion of this they turned to Envestors. Having already raised £500,000 from Envestors in their first fundraising round, they knew it would be a success, and second time around they raised £300,000. Since PRL had reached all of its targets from the first round of funding, the team of investors was happy to get involved again as they knew the company was reliable and could be trusted to reach its goals.

The angel market is now changing and there has been a steady rise in the concept of angel syndicates and investor groups, which are started by experienced angel investors who collect their friends and other investors around them. Examples of this include www. cambridgeangels.com, www.cambridgecapitalgroup.co.uk, www. archangelsonline.com, www.parequity.com and www.angels4angels. co.uk. Usually their business model is that the investors pay for the costs of running the syndicate and entrepreneurs present for free, although there may be charges made for arranging the actual investment.

The trade association for business angel networks in England, Wales and Northern Ireland is the UK Business Angels Association (www.ukbusinessangelsassociation.org.uk), and in Scotland you can find syndicates and networks via LINC Scotland (www.lincscot.co.uk).

In the last few years, a number of new networks have been set up on the web. Effectively they sit between traditional networks and crowd funding platforms, taking advantage of the marketing potential of publicising deals on the web, but not going so far as actually arranging the fundraising itself. One example is https://angel.co/ which is growing rapidly in the US but is also used by lots of UK investors and entrepreneurs.

We are now seeing much more sophistication in the angel market. There are a large number of clubs where the investors join together and get to know each other long before they invest. These clubs are normally managed by a person or business who makes sure that investors are properly looked after before, during and after the investment. As part of their work they find investment opportunities, work with the entrepreneur to create a deal that will be attractive to the investors, organise the fundraising and manage it after the investment has been made. If you are an entrepreneur, you will do a lot of work upfront before the deal is presented to the investors, but with the best clubs you will find that if they commit to the deal, the manager and the investors will definitely ensure that the investment is made.

At the other end of the scale, there has been a rise in the number of networks using the web to help companies raise money. Usually they show profiles of companies looking to raise money (sometimes these look and feel very like fundraising on a crowd platform!) and invite investors to get in touch with the company direct.

When I surveyed the crowd about the platforms they are using to invest, I was interested to find that many people mentioned websites that I would have previously seen as online versions of a typical angel network. It appears that many investors interpret crowd funding as the joining together of a number of different investors to fund an investment opportunity, and therefore these websites count as crowd funding platforms in their minds. I expect that more and more angel networks will build up their skills in presenting fundraising in a more "crowd-like" way in the future, such as including the use of videos and live interaction between fundraisers and investors during the fundraising process. One of the ways in which they will try to keep their offer different will be by organising live meetings of investors and entrepreneurs.

Other things to think about when choosing a platform

You may think that the primary thing to think about when choosing which platform to use is the type of funding the platform can deliver for you, but there is also a number of other, equally important, things to consider.

Flexibility of service

Different platforms offer very different levels of flexibility for a fundraiser. Make sure you opt for one that gives you the flexibility you need, e.g. the ability to change reward offers during a campaign, a flexible campaign timetable, or the option to still take money even if you do not meet your fundraising target (and also if you exceed it).

Finding a site that is suitable for you

The great thing about crowd funding is that it gives both fundraisers and entrepreneurs choice in the type of money handed over. For some companies, raising equity (i.e. selling shares for cash) is the route to go. For others it is raising a loan, and for some it will be getting pledges against rewards – often the reward will be sending the donor one of the finished products that have been made with the money given. I will talk a lot more about this in Chapter 6.

The size of funds required and the time taken to raise them

Different platforms have seen very different rates of success in the amounts that can be raised on them. Kickstarter is notorious for being the platform on which Pebble raised over $10.5m. In stark contrast, www.crowdfunder.co.uk is pretty successful at raising sums of under £5,000.

Fees

Although most platforms take fees of around 5%–9% for themselves and then only on successful fundraising events, there is more variety than you think in what fees you and your investors will pay to meet each other through the crowd. For example, www.sponsume.com charges 4%, and some donation/charitable platforms charge as little as 2.9%. MarketInvoice charges 1% to the fundraiser and takes 20% of investors' profits. You may find that there are other fees too. Some equity funding sites make an additional charge for the legal support they provide, i.e. for all the legal documents and for having a lawyer check everything over to make sure it is watertight once the deal has closed. You also have to remember that whichever organisation processes your payments (e.g. Amazon Payments or PayPal) will take around 1%–3% of the money you raise as processing fees.

One novel feature of crowd funding compared with other types of fundraising is that the fees/commissions charged can vary depending on whether you reach your goal or not. Some platforms such as Kickstarter have one fee based on an "all or nothing" approach. This means that if you fail to reach your goal you don't pay any fees, *but* you also do not get any of the money raised either – it is returned to the investors. Others, such as IndieGoGo, have one fee if you meet or exceed your goal, but they also offer a "keep it all" for fundraisers who do not meet their goal but do raise some money. Typically the "keep it all" money has a higher fee/commission as a percentage of funds attached to it than "all or nothing" fundraisings on the same platform. Never has the idiom "you pays your money and takes your choice" been more true than in the crowd.

When you are fundraising, make sure you understand what the fully loaded cost of your fundraising will be, not least because any fees or commissions that are charged will be taken out of the money raised by the platform operator before the money is handed over to you. You will never see it in your own bank account. So remember to plan for this when preparing your financial forecasts or you may find you are caught short.

Bear in mind that, although it may appear that the fundraiser is paying the costs of using a platform, the fees, commissions and other charges associated with the fundraising are typically taken out of the money pledged by the funders. So in a sense it is the funders who are really paying for the fundraising costs. Not all funders will fully appreciate the implications of this, but you can be sure that the smarter ones will be checking your cash flow projections to make sure you have taken it into account in your costs projections. And whilst a 5% success fee may not seem to be very much money in a £25,000 campaign, in a £1m campaign, it will mean that the fundraiser will not see £50,000 of the cash raised. £50,000 is a lot of money, in absolute terms, to a small business or project. A final thing to think about, whether you are a fundraiser or a funder, is what the total costs of a fundraising might be on different platforms. Whilst one platform may have a cheaper headline fee, if there are a lot of other charges (e.g. for legal documentation), it may end up being a more expensive platform than one whose headline charges are the only ones you will face. Take some time to run the maths based on the charging structures on a variety of platforms to see which will be the most cost effective option for your particular fundraising – you may well be surprised!

Size, type and openness of funder base

Different platforms have very different numbers of investors registered with them. Kickstarter has two million registered pledge-givers – the Pebble watch company raised pledges from over 68,000 funders in its campaign on the platform last year. Crowdcube has around 35,000 registered investors, but some specialist sites may have only a few hundred really big hitters. The number of registered investors does not matter as much as whether they will be interested in you during your campaign. Don't be scared to ask questions of the platform operator about how active investors are and what they actually invest in. Do some analysis of the characteristics of the average type of funder on the platform. There is no point in creating a campaign that needs £10,000 from each funder if the typical person using that site provides only £1,000.

When it comes to crowd funding, it is essential that you realise that not all crowds are the same. I have devoted Chapter 9 to this subject later in the book, but for now you should be aware that there are really only two main types of crowd: those who know you *before* you start fundraising (your inside crowd) and those who do not know you *until* you start your campaign (your outside crowd). For now, the main point I would like you to take away is that whatever platform you choose for your campaign, you should make sure that it is very easy for your inside crowd to register with it so they can back your campaign when it starts.

ThinCats statistics

ThinCats has published statistics about lending on its platform. It now has 1,843 lending members. 145 loans have been made worth £30.8m. Two of these loans have already been fully repaid, with an average interest rate of 11%. Six of the borrowers have had difficulties in meeting the repayment schedule and an extended repayment schedule has been agreed unanimously by the lending syndicate in all cases, and one of these has since repaid its loan. In each of these cases, lenders get an extra 2% interest until the loan is paid off. Two borrowers have entered into administration. The first stage of its secondary market is now up and running.

Conclusion

It would not surprise me if by the end of 2013 there are around 1,000 crowd funding platforms up and running around the world. Some will be very specialised, others will be generalist. Some will be focused on one country, others will be trying to reach the global market place. More traditional fundraising businesses will "adopt" crowd funding platform characteristics. Therefore the choice for both fundraisers and donors/ investors will be incredible.

As always, when you get involved in crowd funding of any type, you should tread carefully, do your research and make sure that you really understand what you are getting yourself into before you start. Do that and you should find joining the crowd a very satisfying and stimulating experience.

In summary

1. There are numerous different types of crowd funding ranging from donation to equity. As well as generalist platforms, there are many very specialist ones.
2. You will always pay a fee to the crowd funding platform – this is usually taken out of the money raised and can range from as low as 2%–3% to 10% or more. Watch out for hidden extra fees.
3. Many types of crowd funding involve continued engagement between fundraiser and donor/investor after the fundraising has taken place, so your fundraising does not end when your campaign is completed.
4. Depending on the type of site, you can raise anything from hundreds to millions of pounds in funding – so choose the site that most suits your cash needs as well as considering other factors.
5. Some fundraising businesses, for example some business angel networks, can also help you raise large sums of money from groups of individual investors, so even if the phrase "crowd funding" is not mentioned, do not necessarily dismiss these people out of hand.
6. Look for a site that has the right level of flexibility for you. Do you want an "all or nothing site", where if you fail to raise your target amount you get nothing? Or do you want one that allows you to keep everything you raise regardless?
7. Understand the size of the crowd you will be talking to on the platform – not just numbers registered, but numbers active and who are likely to be actively interested in you!
8. Make sure the platform you choose makes it easy for your inside crowd to register and back you.
9. Do plenty of more general research. Before you start, look closely at whether fundraising or donating via the platforms you are using really is right for you!

10. New crowd funding platforms are getting going all the time – keep refreshing your research to see which platform is best for you right up to the time your campaign starts. Remember that you don't necessarily need to use the same platform over and over again, especially if your fundraising needs change over time.

Chapter 2

What makes crowd funding different?

The new crowd in town

As you will see from the history of crowd funding in Appendix II, crowd funding is in some ways only the latest development in the market for businesses raising cash to use. In its current format, though, because it is new, it is controversial.

Probably the main reason why crowd funding is so controversial is that it is challenging the established ways of raising money such as bank lending, venture capital or angel investment, or a stock market listing. Established organisations in the market – whether they are lenders or investors – are finding it very challenging to adjust to the arrival of the new crowd in town. In particular, the idea that individuals can bypass banks to borrow money directly from other individuals with money flies in the face of all the principles of how societies control how money moves around the market. Many people operating in the early stage investment world are extremely nervous of websites where entrepreneurs and investors can meet and do business without the checks and balances that come with fundraising or investing via an established network syndicate or intermediary such as a corporate finance firm.

There are also many issues around how regulation works in this new crowd world. Historically, regulation has been about trying to protect people from making investment mistakes by controlling who does what and when. In the crowd world, the whole ethos is reversed and anyone can do what they like when they like.

The other big issue for the traditionalists is about accountability after the fundraising. It's often challenging for a small company that has raised equity fundraising from one or two angels or venture capitalists to keep shareholder relations sweet; what, the traditionalists ask, is going to happen when you have 200 investors, in terms of channelling information to them and in getting decisions from them when the need arises?

However, we are already seeing that the banks are responding well to this new competition. In the case of Zopa, some banks have embraced the platform and have used it to offer loans themselves. Relative newcomer MarketInvoice is increasingly forming partnerships with banks to take on the non-mainstream invoice financing opportunities that the banks cannot fund.

Crowd equity fundraising is very challenging to investors, especially business angels and venture capitalists who have been used to operating in a very tight, illiquid market, where the shares they have bought are extremely difficult to sell. For businesses it can also be difficult in that their fundraising leaves them with a permanent shareholder base that cannot be removed without the permission of those individuals. Essentially you are stuck with each other once the investment has been made. Many venture capitalists and business angels prefer to invest in companies alone or with only a very tight-knit group of fellow investors so that it is easier for them to help the company. Often, companies that fundraise will go through ups and downs that mean shareholders have to make difficult decisions quickly, including providing emergency funding when times are tough. They are understandably nervous when faced with a situation where their fellow shareholders may not fall in line quickly to support a company.

Crowd funding makes investors nervous because typically it is much quicker than other sources of money. It often involves cash being given by many more individuals and, perhaps most importantly of all, it is the most public way you can raise the profile of both your business and its financial requirements, if it is going to grow. In other ways it is hard to see crowd funding as distinct, although there are some projects where crowd funding is more likely to be successful than other types of funding. In particular, crowd equity funding probably works better for start-up and early stage businesses. It is also better for projects in some sectors rather than others – it is especially good for consumer goods and services and creative projects. In contrast, it is probably less suitable for projects in a highly specialised sector, for example, or for those that require a great deal of confidentiality until launched. If you have a small project (i.e. less than £20,000), pledge funding is definitely the way to go, especially if you can give a reward to the funders within the costs of the fundraising.

Some people imagine that crowd funding is only for raising small amounts of money and that it is better to use other sources of funding if you need large sums, but there are now plenty of examples of companies and projects that have raised £1m or more via crowd funding. Examples include Kammerlings, which has raised over £1m in total on Crowdcube via two fundraisings (see page 19), and the ubiquitous Pebble watch, which raised over $10m on Kickstarter (see page 15). So you cannot assume that crowd funding is only for small start-ups.

Whatever nervous investors or others think or say crowd funding is now here to stay and is firmly part of the fundraising ecosystem. Therefore, here is an explanation of how it differs from the more established sources of funding.

Personal, friends and family funding

Nearly every business or project raises the initial money it needs either from the founder's own funds or from money provided by friends and family.

One of the great advantages of crowd funding is that it provides a very easy way to raise money from friends and family. They just go onto the relevant website and apply like everyone else. Another advantage is that it provides a proper discipline for fundraising. Crowd funding sites require the fundraising to be properly organised so friends and family get a complete picture of the opportunity and all the necessary background information – from the business plan to the financials –

so they can make a more informed judgement before they invest or donate. They also have the advantage of investing based on a proper legal framework – the crowd funding platform will automatically ensure, for example, that their shares are properly registered and issued. If it is available, they also get EIS relief. If they lend to the business, they have the advantage of their loans being properly registered and having interest and capital payments made and recorded. When it comes to debt funding and pledges on sites such as Kickstarter, there is a potential advantage in that you can provide the money anonymously, which has the benefit of reducing tensions if things go wrong later on.

The main disadvantage of friends and family using platforms to back entrepreneurs is that there will be standard fees chargeable on the money they provide. However, given that, if they were investing properly, they would have had to get legal advice and incur other costs, it is probably safe to say that using a platform still works out cheaper than investing the traditional way.

Debt funding

With such a variety of debt funding on offer from crowd platforms, entrepreneurs can now explore the potential of borrowing to fund the growth of their business in a way that has never happened before. With bank lending so hard to obtain at the moment, the biggest difference with crowd lending is that it is available at all. The second difference is that it is now very, very quick to borrow – on most platforms a loan will be funded within a couple of days, if not sooner.

Case study

The Space Studio

The Space Studio was founded 12 years ago and has grown steadily since that point. A RIBA-registered architecture and interior design practice, it is based in central Birmingham and offers contemporary new build architectural, refurbishment and commercial interior design services, including the obtaining of appropriate planning permissions.

Its portfolio spreads across residential and commercial sectors into affordable housing and extra-care developments, higher and further education establishments, retail developments and the hospitality and leisure sector. In addition, the Space Studio won a contract to design a new hotel above the refurbished New Street Station in Birmingham, which is a huge boost to their credibility in the highly competitive larger contract market. The directors approached a major high street bank for additional working capital, but the bank was slow even to find a manager to deal with their request. The company turned to ThinCats and sponsor Ludgate Finance to help it find the funding to support its growth. The funds were used partly to repay an overdraft and partly to fund the working capital needs of the business, which is expanding rapidly. The Space Studio was provided with £100,000 over five years at 9.07% interest (weighted average of lender rates). Managing director Kevin Singh is thrilled with the experience, saying:

"It was refreshing to find someone who was more flexible and less risk averse than the mainstream banks. We needed funding to support our expansion due to a large project and the ThinCats process was not only fast and efficient but we were literally inundated with offers from investors!"

In many ways, though, crowd lending bears many similarities to traditional bank lending. Interest rates in particular are set by the crowd in a bidding process to reflect the risk they are taking; currently rates are usually in the mid to high teens. The bidding process comprises each lender putting up a notice on the platform saying how much they are prepared to lend at what interest rate, e.g. £15,000 at 15% for five years. The platform then calculates the different offers and lets the borrower know which is best (note: this might be more or less automatic depending on the platform). The borrower then selects the best offer and the deal is struck. Lending periods (the length of time it takes to repay the loan) are also similar, and you have to meet the arrangement fees charged by the platform as you would do with bank fees. Platforms also require significant financial information so they can assess your ability to repay the loan, and will perform credit and other checks to work out whether you and/or your company are worth lending to. Some platforms such as ThinCats also take security over the loan, which may include your home; if you fail to repay the loan they will then take ownership of these assets and sell them to recoup the money that has been lent to you.

As with normal bank lending or alternative types of borrowing such as factoring, you have to meet all repayments of interest or capital on time or risk a foreclosure on the loan, with all the usual consequences.

Angel funding

Raising funding from angels has become very popular for many ambitious smaller businesses, especially since the credit crunch has made it much more difficult to raise loans from banks, and also, in the UK, because of the attractive tax breaks on offer to UK taxpayers if they invest in shares. Angels will typically invest between £10,000 and £100,000 in a business. Some will have only two or three investments of this size, while others could have 30 or more. While it is true that there has recently been a rise in the number of angels able to invest £1m or more in a business – the so-called "super angels" (who have usually sold a business they founded for a large sum of money) – they are still very much the exception rather than the rule, and you would be wise not to pin all your hopes on finding one for your business.

The traditional route for entrepreneurs and angels to find each other is through a mixture of live networking and using the internet (e.g. via LinkedIn), through investment clubs such as Cambridge Angels (www.cambridgeangels.com) and Par Equity (www.parequity.com), and via the rise of connecting websites such as www.angelinvestmentnetwork.co.uk.

The process of finding investment is time-consuming and not often standardised, with each deal being taken on its own merits by investors. It is largely the responsibility of the entrepreneur to keep looking for enough investors until the funds needed have been raised, and therefore the general rule is to allow six to nine months to raise angel finance. It is quite usual for entrepreneurs to raise finances not from one angel but from many. Unless you are looking for a very small sum, you should expect to end up with at least a handful of angel investors to get all the money you need.

Angels often like to be involved in the businesses they back. They may take a board seat or at the very least have the right to be an observer at board meetings (i.e. prior to the meeting they can put questions to the board and at the meeting they can watch but not contribute). Often they get operationally involved at some point in the company's life, perhaps helping with sales and marketing or in building the supply chain or the production facilities. If you can get angels with this type of expertise and who are willing to get involved with your business, then that is going to be a big win and one worth aiming for.

At the moment, angels have strong views on crowd funding and you can expect them to be a bit nervous if you try to raise money from them at the same time as undertaking an equity crowd funding campaign. The typical worries they have are listed below.

- The crowd might get too excited about your fundraising and overvalue your company, which will mean they get a worse deal. An overvaluation can cause serious problems later on when you want to raise more money from angels or venture capitalists, who would normally value it at a much lower price.
- You will face problems after the fundraising as you try to look after dozens if not hundreds of shareholders and, for example, have to keep them informed about developments. They will also worry that these investors will turn to them for help in dealing with you if problems do arise!
- There is the risk that they will end up being fellow shareholders with people who do not understand about investing in small early-stage businesses.

So, if you are thinking about raising angel funding, have your arguments ready about why you are choosing them as a source of money either before, during or after your crowd funding campaign. Of course, angels will be much less worried if you raise extra money via a pledge or debt route rather than via equity!

Thoughts on crowd funding by an angel

This is what one angel wrote to me when I asked for his thoughts on crowd funding.

1. Many angels are sceptical about crowd sourcing

That's (in part) because we know how much can go wrong in a start-up and how many things need to go right in order for investor(s) to make money. And many of those "right" factors are predicated on a close working relationship between management and shareholders.

That being said, just as angels often band together, with one or a subset of the angels taking a lead role, there is a general two-tier model for start-up funding. With the lead angel(s) doing (most of) the work, the "tier 2" angels are actually riding along. Sometimes there is a payment structure in place to reflect the differential contribution and responsibility of tier 1 versus tier 2. For instance, tier 1 can receive additional options, a percentage of tier 2's profits (above a certain level), or a cash payment for time and materials, post-funding. In many cases professional angel groups simply treat this as a swings-and-roundabouts equation, which nets out automatically over time.

In this perspective and model, crowd sourcing could fit in as an "extreme tier 2", particularly alongside tier 1 angels of repute!

Moreover, there's nothing stopping tier 2 (crowd investors) from doing a little bit of investigative work before they punt, say, £10,000 (or perhaps more, once they've enjoyed some success with a particular tier 1) on a given tier 1 "horse".

2. Exit and dividends

Some people worry about how crowd investors might get their money back. Fact is, most start-ups should be built to fit into existing companies, not to be long-term stand-alone enterprises.

They are what I call injection businesses. As a crowd (or angel) investor, you get paid for your contribution to an injection company when it is sold to its "addressee".

In a few cases, however, the start-up is indeed destined to become a stand-alone enterprise, because that's how its ecology works. In such cases there's limited exit potential for anyone. But that need not matter. The company could continue to grow, hopefully at a decent clip and with decent margins, and become cash generative, perhaps at a fairly early stage. (I have a couple of those in my portfolio.) Provided that founders/managers exhibit a modicum of "straight-laced-ness", there is no reason why the crowd fundee couldn't enjoy such a dividend stream!

Things to think about

If you are confused about whether to take the traditional angel route or the crowd funding one, these are the things to think about.

- How web savvy are you? If you know nothing about the web and especially social media, you will find crowd funding very challenging and should probably look at the angel route.
- How consumer friendly is your proposition? If you are fundraising for a product or service that will sell to the general public (as opposed to business), then the crowd is the perfect place to fundraise. If your product is going to be sold to a business or is very technical, you may find it is better to try angels first.
- How big is your inside crowd and how web savvy is it? If your inside crowd is very small (i.e. under 500 people), you should probably not bother with crowd funding until you have grown it. Note: this is less of an issue if you are planning to borrow money via the crowd. Typically, the debt platform investors are strangers to you and will not be affected in their decision to back you by whether they know you or not.

Crowd equity has revolutionised the selling of shares to raise investment for a business. Project- or donation-based crowd funding has revolutionised the market too, because it now enables entrepreneurs to raise funding to develop a new product or project without selling any shares at all! The big differences in practical terms are numerous. Firstly, there is a standardised approach to funding, including the (typically) much shorter timescale (sometimes as short as a few days) for the fundraising. Other advantages include the ready availability of standard legal documentation compared with angel funding, where each deal will have its own unique documents. With crowd equity you are likely to get many more shareholders (by a factor of 10 or even more) than if you choose the angel route. In addition, with many angel deals you will end up with one or more of your angels becoming involved in the company at board (director) level and possibly in the management of the company. With crowd equity you can expect most of your investors to be passive, letting you get on with the job without regular involvement from them.

At the moment it tends to be true that in equity crowd funding, an entrepreneur can get a higher valuation for their business when they raise money than they might by seeking investment through more traditional routes. There have not been enough fundraisings to do any deep analysis yet, but some of the reasons for this are thought to be:

- Crowd investors are more naïve and therefore accept the higher valuations
- Crowd investors are less bothered about the valuation because they are investing small sums so it does not really matter to them
- There may be a fundamental truth that a company that is prepared to "go public" with its fundraising really may be worth more, as it benefits from the publicity associated with the fundraising and will enable the company to make more sales etc.

Crowd funding fees do not differ much from those charged by advisers who help entrepreneurs raise angel finance. The end results from both angel and crowd equity funding are the same in the sense that the business owner will end up with a number of fellow shareholders in the company. These shareholders will have the same general rights and obligations whichever route you choose, including rights under the UK Companies Act 2006 or any similar legislation in other countries.

One of the interesting things about crowd equity is that it might change the dynamics of how entrepreneurs and investors exit from their businesses, as having a large shareholder base almost automatically invites the company, when it gets large enough, to seek a stock market listing for its shares so people who want to get out can sell – and, indeed, new people who want to get in can buy not only new shares but also shares from existing shareholders. So while angels traditionally have sought to get their exits via a trade sale or, very occasionally, by selling out to a venture capital investor when the latter wanted to invest in the business, with crowd funding the option of flotation is open to them from day one.

Venture capital

Like angels and crowd equity investors, venture capitalists also buy shares in a company in return for a cash investment. Unlike crowd equity, you can expect to have only one or perhaps a small handful of venture capital investors in your company. Those investors are likely to buy shares that carry many more rights for them and obligations for you, and they are also likely to invest part of their cash using a loan instrument on which you will pay interest. Venture capitalists typically invest millions of pounds in any one business. It is noticeable that some are already investing in crowd funding platforms. Raising money from venture capitalists usually takes months and months, as they will want to investigate whether they should invest in you and watch to see how your business is growing.

You can expect venture capitalists to be heavily involved in your business both before and after they invest. They will look very deeply into the business at all times and actively contribute to discussions on how it should be managed. Before they invest they will make lengthy and deep investigations into you, your business and your competitors. They will make calls to third parties, including your customers and suppliers, challenge you on your plans, your numbers and the strength of your team, and take up a lot of your time.

This is both their great advantage and disadvantage. The advantages particularly lie in the fact that they will (probably) have seen it all before and therefore can help you avoid making mistakes, and because they often have an unrivalled network of contacts that can help you grow your business, and therefore their investment, much quicker. They also have the experience to help you achieve a sale of your business when the time is right, which will help you to capitalise in cash terms on all the effort you put into growing the business. The disadvantages include the fact that they will be very involved in decision making, probably holding the purse strings on any major expenditure the company makes. You will also find that, if you do not perform in line with their expectations or if you fall out in a major way, they will have the right to remove you from the business and replace you with someone else.

Flotation

Floating your company on a stock exchange these days is probably only an option for companies that are far larger than any company that would consider crowd funding. Recent floats on the London Stock Exchange have typically been of companies worth hundreds of millions or even billions of pounds. Even AIM, the Stock Exchange's junior market, normally only works for businesses raising millions of pounds and that are properly up and running with good revenues, and ideally with profits being generated year in, year out. However, there are times in any economic cycle when a bubble develops, and it is possible for start-ups with a great plan and a whizzy business idea to float on a listed market, so you should never say never when it comes to finding investment via a flotation. Nevertheless, I would not hold out much hope for a flotation as the answer to your funding problem any time soon – the last time several start-ups were able to float was the dotcom boom at the turn of the century and there is no sign that the stock markets around the world are likely to be receptive to start-ups again any time soon.

Flotation is a very specialised way to find money. Although it also involves raising money from strangers, like crowd funding, and PR is a major factor in a successful round, it is in fact very different. You need specialist advisers including lawyers, accountants, corporate financiers and stock brokers to help in the fundraising. The costs are much higher than those for crowd funding and once the company is listed there are much more onerous responsibilities for the directors of the company (i.e. you) regarding reporting to your shareholders and the market more generally on what the company is doing and how it is performing against expectations. With a large flotation you can also expect lots of analysts to write independent reports on the fundraising and whether it is a good idea or not. These people will also write about your company after the flotation and recommend whether or not people should buy, sell or hold shares in your business. It takes up a lot of management time just dealing with the issues relating to being quoted, let alone running the business.

In summary

1. Crowd funding is controversial: for every evangelist there will be someone who thinks it is a terrible thing.
2. Traditionalists are nervous about crowd funding for many reasons, including the perceived lack of formal regulation, the risks of investors suffering from fraud, the risks for entrepreneurs in having the wrong people influencing their business, and many others.
3. The relationship between fundraisers and donors/investors will be very different if you undertake crowd funding than if you go for more traditional types of finance.
4. Traditional banks, venture capital investors and advisers are already partnering with parts of the crowd. Expect this connectivity to continue.
5. Timing is everything: crowd funding can be very quick, but there are fears that the long-term consequences of running a campaign could be worse than from using traditional funding routes.
6. Bank lending typically takes much more time than borrowing via the crowd, but you do have certain protections because banks are heavily regulated and are obliged to behave in specific ways. If you do find a good

bank manager, he or she could become your cheapest and best business adviser ever.

7. Angel investing differs from crowd funding in that one or more investors may get very involved indeed in your business on a day-to-day basis. They may even take a board or management role. In the crowd, the involvement of funders is likely to be much more remote and communication is more likely to be via online channels such as posts and email.

8. Venture capitalists often invest millions, not hundreds of thousands, of pounds in a company. So the big difference is that if you are successful in raising venture capital money, you are likely to get a much larger sum than the crowd (whether equity or debt) will finance. Venture capitalists are *really* involved in your business and are very powerful.

9. Flotation appears to be a bit like crowd funding, as it also involves lots and lots of investors investing in your business, but in reality it is very different indeed – not least because there will be a public price put on the value of your shares every day and that price may not be to your liking!

10. Unless you are raising a small sum (i.e. less than £50,000), do not dismiss other sources of funding out of hand. Crowd funding is definitely not for everyone.

Chapter 3

Dealing with the doubters

Innovation in any market will cause a major reaction by the established players in that market, and crowd funding is no exception. Since I started telling people that I was writing this book, I have had loads of phone calls from people quietly telling me why they are worried by crowd funding. To put it in context, the vast majority of their worries are in relation to crowd equity sites, but it is fair to say that many of their concerns are relevant in the context of other types of crowd funding.

These comments are typical of the sorts of negative things people told me about crowd investing in my survey.

> "I am not a fan of debt crowd funding as there are all sorts of issues regarding the expectations of the lender (meaning that due diligence on the project creators needs to be quite rigorous)."

> "'Equity' crowd funding is not a great concept, as I believe that equity is the wrong instrument for many high-tech companies or any company requiring more than one round of financing. It seems clear to me that new instruments for crowd investing are required."

Some worry about the funders and others worry about the fundees, but given the strength of feeling among many of them and the genuine doubts they have, it is important that we take a look at them and argue the case. It is well worth understanding the feelings of the doubters as you may come across them during your campaign. I recommend you have your own arguments ready to counter theirs. You never know, you might even turn them into your champions if you argue with them effectively.

In order to create some logic to the concerns, I have grouped them below under a variety of headings.

There are no policemen

Take a walk down any high street. Consider the gambling market, the trading of stocks and shares, putting money in or borrowing it from the bank – everywhere you go there are all sorts of rules and regulations in place to ensure that the transaction that takes place is "proper". If goods are bought, they must be what was described; if you bet and win you must be paid your winnings; if you are sold something in the financial services sector you should expect to get what you paid for and not be mis-sold. In the area of business funding the principal UK regulator is now the Financial Conduct Authority (FCA) (its counterpart in the US is the SEC). The FCA has legions of rules to try to protect investors and ensure that people involved in business and businesses involved in personal finance behave properly.

The worry among the established players is that the crowd funding world has insufficient protections for funders/investors from rogues wanting their money, and for entrepreneurs from rogue funders and investors looking to exploit their nascent businesses. They think this because some parts of the crowd funding market are so new that there has been no time to establish overall rules for best practice, either at a national or at an international level.

I think the worries of the established players in this context are now unfounded. Although the crowd funding world caught everyone from regulators to governments off guard at first, because the nature and scale of the internet suddenly opened funding opportunities to billions of people, governments have in fact been pretty quick to react. In the US, the Obama administration introduced the JOBS Act; which is gradually being brought into force by the Securities and Exchange Commission (SEC). The JOBS Act effectively legalises all crowd funding activity. In the UK, both platform operators and the government have reacted swiftly to this issue of governance. Crowd equity platforms such as www.seedrs.com are typically seeking and obtaining FCA authorisation and those that have not yet done so are working closely with accountancy and legal firms to make sure that they are abiding by the law. The UK debt funding platforms have been even more proactive. They have gone so far as to push the UK government to build a new framework of regulation, so that everyone involved in debt crowd funding has to operate in line with best practice. At the time of writing we are still waiting for the first proposals to emerge for public discussion and debate.

Of course, the ultimate policeman in the crowd is the crowd itself. At a commercial level the crowd is deciding for itself which opportunities are worth funding. As there is no intermediary "punting" the opportunity, there is no one who has a commercial interest in getting a bad project funded. Funders can readily use the internet to check out fundraisers to see if they are good guys or bad guys. The debt platforms in particular have put in place lots of checks and balances to try to prevent people from raising loans that will not be repaid. The fact that they reject so many of lending applications suggests that they have their due diligence well in hand.

There have been instances of pledge funding that have taken the money and failed to fulfil the pledges they promised, but these are few and far between and it all gets pretty public, as you can see from the case study below. As time moves on I think we can expect the crowd to get more and more sophisticated at working out which of the opportunities they are offered will be the winners and which will be the losers.

Case study

ZionEyez

ZionEyez started on Kickstarter and proposed to produce glasses under the brand name "Eyez" that could stream real-time high definition video and audio to the internet from a built-in camera and microphone in the frame of the specs. They were offering people the chance to own a pair of these revolutionary glasses for the low price of just $199. They had set a target of $55,000, and on 31st July 2011 – the closing date – they had succeeded in reaching and exceeding that, raising $343,415 from over 2,000 backers. They intended to ship their product to their backers during the winter of 2011. After updating their Kickstarter page for a few months and promising new developments, nothing appeared and backers started to get angry. With most giving up their investment as a loss, and some threatening legal action, the ZionEyez team then stopped updating the page and nothing has been heard from the founders on the Kickstarter page since 10th April 2012. In an interview with www.geekwire.com, Matt Krumholz, Vice Chairman of Zion Eyes said the team was evolving and that silence did not signify a lack of progress. People that had pre-ordered through the Zion Eyes site have been refunded.

Does it actually work for most?

With all the noise, it is easy to miss the fact that many people and businesses who want to use crowd funding sites to raise money fail. Kickstarter's statistics suggest that fewer than 50% of campaigns succeed, and, as I mentioned above, many of the lending sites will reject over 80% of loan applications. Some of the people who fail to fundraise go back to the drawing board, rework their campaign and are then successful the second time around, but it is already clear that crowd funding is not a panacea for everyone and that if you are going to be successful you have to take it as seriously as any other fundraising *route*.

Meanwhile, traditional sources of funding such as angels and venture capitalists are having to up their game. Increasingly, angel networks are specialising at what they do. Angels tell me, for example, that London Business Angels is increasingly becoming the go-to network for medical technology start-ups, and many of the angels are joining or forming for themselves club-type arrangements where the angels co-ordinate themselves prior to, during and after a fundraising so the whole process becomes less random. Here in the UK we are also seeing more and more venture capitalists build formalised relationships with angels – a good example is Octopus Venture Partners, which comprises over 100 angels who co-invest with the Octopus Investments capital fund managers. Indeed, the Octopus ventures team typically only invests in a deal once the partners have said that they want to invest.

The banks are also looking harder at how they will behave in a world where the crowd does the job that used to be exclusively theirs. For example, the bank manager for my own business, AngelNews, works very hard to give me a lot of support around the business's funding needs and strategy, which is the sort of support that may not be on offer if I did a crowd borrowing campaign. I suspect that we will see a big change in the way banks look after their customers as the banks' management teams realise that their businesses will be under threat if they don't become more customer-friendly.

As a funder, I won't get what I was promised

There is incredible variety in terms of how different types of crowd funding perform from the investor's perspective. It ranges from pretty much a 100% success rate in getting your money back (and more) from invoice auction sites such as MarketInvoice, to a certain amount of failure of loans on debt platforms (though according to the industry, this is within market norms). In the social funding world, sites such as Kiva have incredibly strong track records of repayment of microloans and the investors are getting great returns on their money as well. In the crowd equity world, we still do not know if the companies raising crowd equity will deliver similar or better returns to angel and venture capital funding, as, to date, no crowd equity fundraiser has yet exited!

If I were to hazard a guess, I would imagine that when crowd funding matures, the returns for debt and equity will not be that dissimilar to the returns seen by traditional debt and equity investors. They may even be better as the crowd gets better at assessing risk. The only note of caution is that, due to the very nature of crowd funding, there are likely to be more really commercially risky propositions on the platforms as the crowd becomes the main place where first-time entrepreneurs and others go. And there will always be surprise failures and unlikely successes – that is why crowd investment is so exciting.

Pledge funding is a bit different to other types of funding because it is not an investment as such. When you make a pledge it is because you are supporting someone to do something interesting and new, or just to be able to do something they could not otherwise do. So in a sense the actual reward you might get is the icing on the cake. According to Kickstarter's statistics, three-quarters of technology and design-related projects aren't finished on time. Anyone doing pledge funding should see their donation in this context. That being said, if you have pledged a considerable sum of money (and arguably anything over a token donation), you should expect to get the reward you are promised. Fundraisers are consistently getting better at improving their donation/rewards combinations as they learn from others who have done campaigns before them. I expect that soon the pledge market will have got so good at this that donors will not have to worry much about whether or not they will get their reward – they just will.

However, there are still many scare stories about campaigns that went wrong. The case of OpenVizsla is interesting. After the event, sceptics might think it was obviously a bit odd and that funders should have steered clear, but then others might say that crowd funding is all about backing the unknown! It would be interesting to know how you would have reacted in the case of OpenVizsla.

Case study

OpenVizsla

In November 2012, a pair of hackers who go by the pseudonyms Pytey and Bushing, known for cracking the code behind Apple's iPhone and Nintendo's Wii, turned to Kickstarter to fund their next project, a dongle that can connect to a device, grab its data and help crack open the system. They set a target of $17,500 to produce and deliver their product – for which they supplied no release date – and within a month raised over $81,000. It was looking like a great success, but the pair underestimated both the amount of interest they would receive and the complexity of putting the device together. Two years down the line, the 584 backers are still leaving comments on the Kickstarter page asking for updates, with most suspecting that their donation has gone forever. A blog posting on the OpenVizsla website says that they are working on extra features and they're hoping to send out prototypes soon.

Giving away the family silver

Crowd funding is public, *very* public. This makes some nervous, especially those used to placing enormous importance on things like business trade secrets. The very spirit of crowd funding is to bare all to anyone who wants to take a look. Inevitably this creates risks, especially for more complex businesses, but equally, in this new world where everyone starts to know everything about us from the day we join Facebook (or before), for a simple business that is brand-based rather than intellectual property (IP)-driven, telling the crowd is a positive marketing advantage rather than a competitive threat. You have to be very speedy in terms of delivery if you fund yourself via the crowd because inevitably your idea is out there for other people to copy. If it is a good idea, I can promise you it *will* be copied, so you have to stay ahead of the competition and think like this from the day you launch your campaign, not the day you launch your product.

In contrast, though, the advantage the crowd brings to many start-ups is that it does not just act as your funder, but also as the place to do your market research and test out customer demand. In the old days you could spend months and tens of thousands of pounds finding out if anyone would buy your product and, if so, what your product should be. Through the crowd you have a much better chance of understanding "on trends", so you can shape your product or service to meet what people really want rather than what you think they want. You can also see what everyone else is doing and therefore make yourself different and better than the rest. If you can use that to stay nimble and innovative there is no reason why you cannot beat the competition.

As it currently exists, the crowd is probably not the place to fundraise for small companies that are not really in a position to protect an attack on their IP, because they don't have a war chest of cash with which to pay lawyers to fight the nasty people who try to steal their secrets or kill them off by copying them. In this case, the doubters who think the crowd is not the place for some businesses are right. As you can see from the case study below, IP disputes can get nasty and big, pretty quickly – and they can involve the most unlikely people.

Words of advice from the expert

IP issues in crowd funding, by Helen Jones, patent attorney at Gill Jennings & Every

A recent news item set alarm bells ringing in the US when Kickstarter was sued for patent infringement.

The well known crowd funding platform was named in a patent dispute alongside one of its most successful fundraising companies, Formlabs, in a matter relating to a 3D printer. The plaintiff, 3D Systems, alleges that a device that was supplied by Formlabs to investors pledging above a specified sum infringed one of its patents that remained in force. Kickstarter's arrangement with its fundraising companies is to retain a percentage of the funds raised on its platform. It acquires no equity, nor does it retain a proportion of sales of products. Critics of the position taken by the patent holder point out that Kickstarter emphasises that it does not act as a sales agent. Exactly what act carried out by Kickstarter is one that infringes the patent is not clear, nor is it certain that the patent owner will be successful if the case comes to trial. No doubt Kickstarter (or its insurers) will be looking to the company for redress and this will inevitably be both time-consuming and expensive for Formlabs to deal with.

I do not know if other crowd funded companies have been sued for patent infringement, or indeed infringement of other IP rights, such as designs or trademarks. Since many have innovative products or services to sell, and since the crowd funding model has had some successes, it seems likely they have. In my view, whether there are any IP risks in the businesses being funded certainly bears consideration. As with any early stage company, some assessment of the competitive landscape and the IP existing there is sensible. If the company makes assertions about its own IP position, and especially its freedom to operate, this can be critically analysed. I have seen statements such as "the technology involved is open source". Take care here, as this may reflect the fact that the company has no intention of enforcing its own IP rights against third parties. Third parties in the space whose business could be affected by the new player in the market and who own their own IP may have an entirely different view of the newcomer's freedom to exploit such rights. The decision whether to invest in IP advice at the point of investing will depend on the amount being invested and the willingness of the investor to take risk. Where equity is being acquired, and a long-term view is taken, it may be worth the investment in taking such advice. Where there is no equity, and a product with a short life or which will not require spares or consumables not readily available from other sources, an investor will sensibly take the view that the IP risk is low in priority.

As a potential fundraiser on one of these platforms, make sure the terms concerning IP rights, if any, are reviewed and understood. They may prohibit infringement and may include indemnities for the funding platform. There is a possibility they may encourage or require open access to any technology. If this is the case, and if IP rights could create high value in the company to be funded, then an alternative way of funding will have to be sought.

Stealing other people's silver

There is one issue that many first-time entrepreneurs are probably not terribly aware of, namely that their great new idea may actually be a copy of something else that already exists. In addition, it can be easy to steal something by accident that actually belongs to somebody else and that they would not normally give you without giving their express permission. A really simple example of this could be revealing details about one of your funders, which might breach the Data Protection Act 1998. It is very easy in the hyper-excited world of the crowd to make mistakes of this type, and, because of the way the crowd works, once done it is there for the entire world to see and pass on. The only solution is to then try to retract what you have done and apologise (and, in a worst case scenario, pay compensation). But the damage will have been done.

So the doubters who are concerned about this issue have good reason. Everyone in the crowd needs to pay serious attention to the issue because it is so easy to make a mistake. Data protection is an even more important issue in the crowd than it is for traditional business. You need to think about how you will password-protect the PCs, tablets and mobiles you use for your campaign and how you will protect the data you end up holding on individuals, especially their contact details and addresses and any financial information you might hold, such as their bank account details.

Who is the crowd anyway?

The internet is amazing because you and other people can now find each other much more easily, but you need to remember that it can also be used to do great damage to you and to other people, as recent controversies around libellous comments circulating via Twitter have highlighted. If you are crowd funding you have to be aware that you must not use it to tell untruths about yourself, about your business and definitely not about other people, or you can expect a (possibly major) reaction. Remember that juicy information on the internet has a nasty way of going viral – this is as true for crowd funding as for other areas such as news. Later on in Part 3, we will talk about whose crowd is it anyway, but it's worth pointing out here that not everyone in the crowd is friendly and some people may not have your best interests at heart. If you are taking money from strangers, especially when you are selling them something as long term as shares in your company, you face a real risk in that you may be taking money from someone you do not like or who does not like you and who may have nefarious intentions that you don't know about. The onus is therefore on fundraisers to understand the risks they are taking and set up procedures to deal with problems if they do arise. The onus is also on you to tell the truth and not fail to give people information that would be relevant to them.

In summary

1. Established people and businesses always worry about new developments in their market – they may take action to try to stop newcomers from succeeding if they feel that their own position or business will be threatened.
2. Crowd funding has become so big so quickly it is not surprising that there are real worries about it.
3. Lots of people are worried about how crowd funding is being policed, even some platform operators!
4. Many in the crowd believe that it will be the crowd funders themselves who become the best policemen.
5. On many platforms more than 50% of campaigns fail to reach their target fundraising, so you should not assume that crowd funding is a dead cert when it comes to getting money.
6. Although relatively rare, there are cases where donors/ investors have not received what they have been promised, so crowd investing is not a dead cert either.
7. Crowd funding is very public and you can assume that all your secrets will become known widely the minute you start a campaign and forever after. So think seriously before you start.
8. Investors and donors can stay hidden, but you should not assume that this will always be the case as the crowd may decide that it wants to find out who you are.

9. Be very careful of crowd funding if you have an idea or project that is very valuable but can be copied relatively easily if people find out your secrets. If you are a business with unique ideas or designs, make sure you speak to a specialist adviser such as a patent attorney before you start your campaign.
10. Remember that you may inadvertently be stealing protected IP from others. If you crowd fund this could get found out very quickly – so make sure you have avoided this trap before you start.

Chapter 4

Setting up your own crowd funding platform

(and other ways to make money out of the crowd funding explosion)

I assume that most of the people who will pick up this book will be doing so either with the aim of getting advice on how to use crowd funding platforms to raise money or on how to invest or donate using one of the many sites now up and running. However, there may be a few who want to glean knowledge on how to set up a platform or how to exploit the business opportunities being created by the crowd funding revolution. Therefore this chapter is devoted to providing some guidance on how to set up a platform and some other ways to earn money from this market.

The financial services sector is one of the few industries that can sustain dozens and dozens of major players in any one sub-segment. Just think about the banking sector, for example, where there are any number of organisations offering banking, lending, saving and investment products and services. There is reason to believe, therefore, that just as many crowd funding platforms will be able to co-exist effectively and profitably.

Research published by Massolution in May 2013 suggested that over one million funding campaigns were successfully funded in 2012, showing a growth of 81% on 2011, and that this will grow enormously over the next couple of years. Around 600 crowd funding sites are thought to be operational around the world; the industry was worth around $2.7bn in 2012 and may grow to $5bn in 2013. (You can find the research at http://www.crowdsourcing.org/editorial/2013cf-the-crowdfunding-industry-report/25107?utm_source=release&utm_medium=text&utm_content=top&utm_campaign=2013CF+Launch.) Given the relative ease with which you can set up a crowd funding platform, I would expect many more to be established over the next few years.

Here are the major things you should think about when setting up a platform.

Identify a niche

Since I started to tell people that I was writing this book, I have received loads of emails from people telling me about the sites they are setting up. There are the mainstream ones, of course – project sites such as Kickstarter, equity sites such as Crowdcube and Seedrs, lending sites ranging from Funding Circle to ThinCats, and social sites such as CrowdMission. But there are also many people setting up more specific sites – one good example is www.thelendingwell.com, which is working on a model that provides crowd funding of payday loans.

Case study

Syndicate Room

Business angels who know each other well have been syndicating their investments to ensure the deal is fully funded for many years, but it is only recently that business angels have started thinking of including 'the crowd' to take part in an investment syndicate. Some angel networks are beginning to work with crowd platforms on an occasional basis, but Goncalo de Vasconcelas has now taken this to a new level with the launch of Syndicate Room. It is the first online platform specifically designed to bring business angels and the crowd together, allowing informed investors to co-invest small amounts of capital with experienced business angels. This new model of finance is called "Syndicate Funding 2.0", a name designed to show that whilst it resembles well proven syndication models, it is actually something new. Syndicate Funding 2.0 addresses the main points of concern that business angels often raise about equity crowd funding.

- *Due diligence – although investors are not liable for each-others' due diligence, the crowd is reassured that the business has passed detailed scrutiny by business angels, who are confident enough to put their own capital into the deal.*
- *Valuation – the valuation is the result of an often tense negotiation between the entrepreneurs and business angels rather than simply set by the entrepreneurs, providing better valuation to the investors.*
- *Post-investment guidance and contacts – business angels are known for adding value in the form of guidance and contacts. Whilst some entrepreneurs may prefer to fly solo, ambitious entrepreneurs tend to appreciate the difference this can make to their own success.*

Interestingly Syndicate Room has seen a very different type of activity from pure equity crowd funding platforms. Members of Syndicate Room tend to be successful professionals looking to invest small amounts into ambitious start ups and business angels looking to build a diversified portfolio knowing that there is already a lead business angel investor in the deal.

Syndicate Room is differentiating itself from other crowd funding platforms particularly in the types of deals that it funds. Retail and deals in other very risky sectors (from an investor's point of view) are rarely to be found on the platform. Early fundraisings also appear to show that deals which are carried on the platform are more likely to close successfully, with the full amount of money they need, than on other ones. The amount of money raised is also larger than the norm – the smallest deal so far has been £400,000 although the platform states that it will accept deals looking to raise as little as £150,000.

If you want to set up a site, the trick is to find a niche where you can offer either a solution that is not yet being exploited or a cheaper, faster or just plain more effective solution than others.

Copying someone else or building something unique

It is rare that anyone builds a crowd funding platform that is totally unique. As a rule, if something truly innovative (such as a new type of crowd funding) takes off in Silicon Valley, from the date it gets going you will have about 18–24 months to launch a copycat business here in the UK and get it up and running. A good example of this is MarketInvoice with its invoice auction model. The co-founders saw the success of The Receivables Exchange (www.receivablesexchange.com) based in the US and brought it to the UK, where the market was unexploited. Platform Black (www.platformblack.com) is also copying the model in the UK.

It is the nature of the web that if you can set something up then so can someone else, so you need to find some differentiating factors and unique selling points (USPs) that make it difficult for others to copy you. In the case of ThInCats, it is trying to have lower default rates for its loans by insisting on taking security to support any borrowings sought. This gives comfort to investors that they are more likely to get their money back even if things go wrong. It is also assessing loans along similar lines to how traditional lenders and investors operate, such as really looking into the people asking for the loan as well as at their businesses.

Build a brand

If you are based in the UK you will have seen the phenomenal success of the insurance comparison website www.comparethemarket.com, which has used its meerkat mascots to build its business with stunning success in recent years. The viral nature of the internet means that creating a powerful brand is vital to success. It goes without saying that behind the brand there should be the business principles and quality of service happy customers expect.

The first step to building a brand is to get a good website URL. Go for one that is instantly recognisable and that "does what it says on the tin". But beware having a URL that is so similar to everyone else's that you will be confused with the masses. And make sure it is a short and catchy name.

Think about the look and feel of the platform. Some colours and fonts automatically bring to mind financial services, others don't. As well as doing your research by looking at other platforms that are up and running, it is well worth taking some advice from an expert in website design.

Get the operational factors right

If you think you can set up a crowd funding platform of any type for just a few thousand pounds, you will be on the wrong course. Having spoken to many UK-based platform operators, it is clear that it costs tens of thousands, if not hundreds of thousands, of pounds to get a really good crowd website up and running effectively. You need to build a site that will operate smoothly and effectively when thousands, if not millions, of people are using it simultaneously. It will need to be able to cope with demands from regulators to monitor what is going on and also from the taxman, who is increasingly looking into how to audit the ways in which investors using these sites are making money.

Behind the website you will need to have not only enough bodies, but, more importantly, properly expert individuals to deal with the inevitable issues that will arise. For example, in the case of many sites in the UK, you will need compliance people who will look after regulatory issues; for debt funding sites, you will need people who can assess loan applications and decide which ones are appropriate for appearing on the site. You will also probably need your own in-house, or as near as possible to in-house, software developers who can quickly update the code behind the site when problems arise. Another area where employing the right talent is vital is in sales and marketing. This will include experts on web marketing, but also people who can do PR and those who already have good networks in place to be on the ground drumming up both fundraisers and investors or donors.

Algorithms and apps

If you think that setting up a crowd platform is all about look and feel, then think again! Because of the nature and scale of crowd funding you need some pretty clever mathematics and software to ensure that it will operate smoothly when thousands or even millions of transactions a day are passing through it. ThinCats spent 18 months developing its algorithms and software before launching, and even now the founder Kevin Caley says they are still working on updates and improvements so that everything runs seamlessly. You will need to keep your developers on board, probably permanently, because just as you think you have got everything working right, you might find yourself being asked by the taxman to incorporate some more functionality so they can check who is earning what on each transaction. He may even require you to deduct his piece of the pie (i.e. tax) at source and pay it straight over to them.

The market is also seeing the development of crowd funding apps, such as the one offered by www.growvc.com. So bear in mind that if you are building a platform, you will need to be able to provide add-ons such as an app: not only because it will provide a better experience for your crowd, but also because if all your competitors have one, you will not be able to afford not to. You need to set aside a reserve for new innovation related to your platform – at any minute the internet may take a great leap forward (did you know the iPad was launched only three years ago?!), leaving you having to spend money to get your platform up to date.

Insurance

For many new businesses, insurance is only necessary at a very basic level in the early days, but with a crowd funding platform you will need to take specialist advice and probably buy a tailored insurance policy to cover you against the specific risks you will be facing. In particular you will need to think about insuring against fraud, regulatory changes and other third party issues that might impact on your ability to trade. Depending on the model you adopt, you may need to insure against the risk of money moving through your platform ending up in the wrong hands.

Regulation, other laws and tax

Not all platforms need to be formally regulated, although the way the market is moving, it is likely that the new Financial Conduct Authority (formerly the Financial Services Authority (FSA)) and the government will bring in more rules and laws to control how platforms work. The equity platform www.seedrs.com has already obtained FSA authorisation and we understand that others are following its lead. The authorities are now paying lots of attention to the debt platforms; in late 2012 it was announced that they will be working with the main operators to establish a regulatory framework for crowd activity. Even pledge sites such as Kickstarter, IndieGoGo and the UK-based www.crowdfunder.co.uk have to comply with the rules set out in the Companies Act, so you would be well advised to employ a lawyer to give you some good advice on this. It may cost some tens of thousands of pounds to get the right advice, so factor that into your start-up costs. It will be money well spent.

Terms of business

Although it may be tempting to look at the terms of business of existing platforms and adapt them for your own platform when you start up, because things can get so big so quickly in the crowd, you should take specialist advice on your own terms of business before you launch and make sure that they are correct. This will probably mean employing a specialist lawyer to ensure that the i's and t's are dotted and crossed.

How will you handle the money?

The vast majority of platforms collect the funds provided by the crowd using global payment systems such as Amazon Payments (https://payments.amazon.co.uk) and PayPal (www.paypal.com). There is a lot to be said for others following suit, but look closely at the other options you may have. Because of the volume of transactions that will go through your platform, it may be cheaper to use alternatives. For example, SagePay (www.sagepay.com) or Google Wallet (www.google.co.uk) may be good options, and for some platforms it may be cheaper and just as effective to set up your own merchant account with organisations such as WorldPay (www.worldpay.com) or Streamline (www.streamline.com).

Funding your platform

Although you will not need a large capital base of your own to fund the businesses or projects on your site, you will need enough capital to finance the business in the first instance and, perhaps more importantly, enough working capital to keep the whole show on the road for a long time – probably until well after you move into early profitability. Existing site owners have told me that they typically spent between £200,000 and £1m getting their businesses up and running. Initially they raised funds from friends and family and from business angels, but it is noticeable that the larger sites have also raised money from venture capitalists – in the case of Funding Circle, it was from Index Ventures.

The great advantage of raising external finance is that it is hard to raise money from savvy angels and venture capitalists, so if you can present an investment case that proves to your investors that the business of platform operation works and it impresses them, this will validate your plan.

Sales, marketing and PR

If there is one case study where a platform has used PR to maximum effect, it is MarketInvoice which appointed a dedicated PR expert and set up co-founder Anil Stocker as the face of the company. Interestingly, when talking to the press, I found that it was not just the noise that MarketInvoice created that has led to it receiving so much coverage, it is also because the business itself is doing something clever and impressive, and because Anil Stocker is a reliable, intelligent commentator on matters relating to banking and debt finance for the SME sector. So, as the founder of your own platform, it is essential that you too can become the face of the site.

Clever use of social media, ranging from Twitter to more traditional routes such as email newsletters, is also essential to success, so make sure you build this into your initial and ongoing marketing strategy. As with all website-based businesses, you need to get your search engine optimisation strategy right too.

When it comes to sales, one day hopefully you will reach nirvana, with both people looking for money and investors signing up of their own accord, but before then you will need to stimulate activity. The use of agents can be very helpful in driving sales. The best agents will already have access to high-quality people and businesses who need money or who can invest. Think about how you will reward them to ensure that they bring the right opportunities to your site.

Business model and cash flow

Platforms have different models for where they take their own payments for the services they provide. These range from sites where they just take a single commission out of the funds raised (e.g. www.seedrs.com) and ones where they take a payment from both sides of the transaction (e.g. www.marketinvoice.com) through to those that raise a variety of supplementary income such as registration fees (www.crowdcube.com) and no doubt commissions for recommending people such as video producers who will help to get your campaign right. You will need to balance for yourself the pros and cons of how you take your fees and whether you can create a competitive advantage by using a charging model that works better for campaigners and funders.

Most crowd funding sites are currently operating business models where they get paid on success and therefore have negative working capital, i.e. they have to deliver (aka spend cash) before they get paid. Therefore, you need to cost fully what you are doing to make sure that when you do get paid you really are profitable. You also need to think about how you collect the money you are owed. Most of the donation-based sites use online payment providers such as PayPal and Amazon, but if you are dealing with large commissions based on equity and debt models you will need to consider how to extract your own fees at the right time. The easiest way to do this is to ensure that before funds are handed over to the recipient you remove your fees. You may need to use a lawyer or accountant regulated to hold client money for this purpose. For debt funding sites in particular, you may also wish to think about whether you take a monthly fee during the course of the loan as well as upfront fees when the loan is funded.

How Seedrs came about

Interviews with the founder Jeff Lynn and his investor Kayar Raghavan

Jeff Lynn – the founder

Why did you set up Seedrs?

We set up Seedrs because we believe there are profound inefficiencies in the market for seed capital, from both the entrepreneur's and the investor's perspectives.

- For entrepreneurs, there are very few ways available to raise true seed capital. Many businesses need £50,000 or £100,000 to build a minimum viable product or take another first step, but this tends to be too small an amount for venture capitalists and too early for angels. The result is that unless an entrepreneur has very wealthy friends and family, or substantial savings, it is nearly impossible to get his or her start-up off the ground. We believe there are tens of thousands of nascent entrepreneurs up and down the country who have the potential to build great businesses but who never even get their foot in the door.

- For investors, the inefficiency is around the minimum amounts one can invest in start-ups. Due to the transaction costs of investing off-line, angel investors can rarely invest less than £10,000 per deal (and often it's £25,000 or more). To build a diversified portfolio – which is necessary in order to generate profits in an asset class with such a skewed distribution of returns – it therefore takes £200,000 or more, not to mention a whole lot of time. This limits angel investing to the top 1% by wealth (and only those members of the top 1% who have the time to devote to making lots of off-line investments). But investable capital is held by the top 20%, and many in the 2%–20% range, whom we call the "mass affluent", would love the opportunity to invest in start-ups. Under the traditional, off-line system, there was simply no way for them to do so.

Seedrs aims to address these inefficiencies by providing a platform for the mass affluent to invest in seed-stage businesses.

How did you come to set up Seedrs?

My co-founder, Carlos Silva, and I began working on it as a business school project. When we realised just how powerful a proposition we had developed, we decided to devote ourselves to it full time. We began work immediately after graduation (in late 2009) and set to designing every detail of the model, building the platform and obtaining regulatory approval. Along the way we raised the capital we needed to get off the ground and recruited a team. We opened to entrepreneurs in May 2012 and launched to investors in July 2012.

What did you do that was different to other crowd funding sites?

Crowd funding is a very broad term and can be (and is) used to apply to a whole host of very different models. In our view, rewards-based sites such as Kickstarter and IndieGoGo are in an entirely different business from equity-based sites such as Seedrs. It's as different as Amazon (where you purchase products, as on Kickstarter) is from E*TRADE (where you make investments, as on Seedrs). So we see ourselves as vastly different from the rewards-based crowd funding platforms out there.

As for other equity-based crowd funding platforms, the main difference is that we stay involved after the investment has been made. We think it's great to have several dozen or several hundred people allocate their capital to – and get involved in – a start-up, but having them be legal shareholders poses problems both to the company and to the investors. To the company, it makes it nearly impossible to raise further capital. And for the investors, there is no one in place looking out for their rights, which substantially increases the chance that, if the company is successful, they won't get to participate in that success. Our nominee structure – through which we hold the shares as legal shareholder, cast votes and issue consents, and then pass proceeds on to the investors – addresses this. In our view, that is an absolutely critical distinction, and it is the key factor in ensuring both that successful businesses can raise more capital and that the investors who invest through the platform will actually see returns from those successful businesses.

How did you go about getting the investment?

We raised our initial capital from friends, family and some small angels; shortly before launch, we raised a big angel round from a variety of prominent financial services and technology investors.

What are you doing with the investment money now?

We are using the capital to employ our team (we have 14 employees working on technological development, investment and marketing), engage in marketing the platform, obtain ongoing legal and compliance advice and handle general administration.

How is Seedrs going so far?

Fantastic – we're now a year in and have funded 30 deals, which we believe is a record for any equity crowd funding platform. Our hypotheses about the gap in the market for seed-stage capital have clearly proven correct, and our model is proving very popular in addressing that gap. We're thrilled with how it's gone so far and look forward to further growth in 2013.

Why did you get FCA (formerly FSA) regulation, and how did you go about getting it?

We got FCA regulation because it is legally required under the Financial Services and Markets Act 2000 (FSMA). The equity-based crowd funding platforms that operate without regulation are doing so illegally. We have always been committed to conducting our business on a fully legal basis, so to us FCA regulation was a necessity from day one.

As for how we obtained regulation, we worked very hard to design and build a model that was consistent with FSMA and

FCA regulations, and we submitted an application to the FCA in April 2011. We then spent 13 months answering the FCA's questions and making small changes to the model at their request, and the FCA authorised us in May 2012.

What do you feel is the future of Seedrs and of crowd funding (both for businesses and for other projects) in general?

We naturally see a very strong future. For Seedrs in particular, we intend to become the go-to place for British (and eventually European) start-ups seeking to raise their first capital, and for investors who want to build a diversified portfolio of start-up investments. And for crowd funding in general, we think that it will become as standard for new businesses and projects to raise initial capital through crowd funding as it is to design a logo or open a bank account.

Do you have an exit strategy?

Our focus for now is on creating value. If we do that successfully enough, there will be ample exit opportunities.

What advice would you give to an entrepreneur looking to fund their business? What types of project are most successful?

The key lesson we have learned is that momentum is everything. An entrepreneur needs to tap his or her own networks to get the first 10%, 20% or even 30% of the capital he or she is seeking in order for independent investors to join. It's important for any entrepreneur to think like an investor, and one of the first things to realise about how investors think is that they only want to participate when they see other people already doing so.

Do you have any other comments about your journey with Seedrs or on your experience with crowd funding in general?

My main observation is that equity-based crowd funding really isn't as revolutionary as it may seem. In many ways it is simply a natural progression of angel investing into a digitised form. The internet has taken lots of activities that used to be available only off-line and created efficiencies by bringing them online, and in many ways equity-based crowd funding is just one more example of that.

Kayar Raghavan – the investor
How did you hear about Seedrs in the first place?

I heard about Seedrs from a friend when we both were at a *Financial Times* seminar.

Why did you decide to invest in Seedrs?

1. I liked the concept of crowd funding in general.
2. I thought the concept was timely given the very low financial help available to entrepreneurs from traditional sources such as banks.
3. I liked the Seedrs founders – this was very important to me.
4. The data and analysis presented to me by Jeff Lynn were believable and cogent.
5. Seedrs' emphasis on getting FSA approval and observing legal and financial discipline, from the start, impressed me.

How did you go about investing in Seedrs?

I studied and researched the business concept. I read the business plan and the data and analysis backing it. I looked at competition. I read about the equity crowd funding efforts in the States and listened to the congressional hearing to understand legal aspects in further detail. I asked for and obtained written clarifications from Jeff on the questions I had on Seedrs' plans. I then met with Jeff over two extended sessions, among others, to see if I was comfortable with him. Once I felt comfortable with Jeff (and Carlos), I decided to invest. Valuation was a consideration but ultimately not that critical as long as it was in line, but as it was not it did have an impact.

What were your expectations of the investment?

My initial expectation was that my investment would provide impetus for other investors to join, as I was an early investor. I increased my own planned investment and ended up leading a syndicate of investors, ultimately.

Why did you decide to get involved in crowd funding?

It is a unique and creative idea and it appealed to me. It is timely in that it plugs a current market inefficiency where credit is no longer available to worthy ideas or causes and capable entrepreneurs. At a time when everything is "social", it is only appropriate that crowd funding (a "social" idea) finds its place therein. It is my belief in crowd funding's ultimate success that made me invest in a platform that promotes it, Seedrs.

How is your investment panning out?

It is still early days, but so far so good. The business is off to a decent start and it is gaining both visibility and traction. I am sanguine about its eventual success as a great idea coming good on its promise.

What do you think about the future of crowd funding?

It will be very successful, but it will be a while before traditionally conservative societies, where equity investing is not the norm, take to it fully. A combination of education and mass marketing will eventually lead crowd funding to its appropriate and prominent place in the fundraising market. The crowd funding industry itself will also change and develop. There will be consolidation, though, and takeovers of some platforms, and other niche players with depth (such as green projects, industry sector specialists and companies with the largest market share in their country) will emerge. There will also be a couple of global players (who will have more breadth rather than depth).

Participating in the industry

As crowd funding has grown, more and more platform operators have seen the benefits of making the market work better. Therefore a number of trade associations have been founded, including the World Crowdfund Federation (www.worldcrowdfund.org), the US-based National Crowdfunding Association (www.nlcfa.org) and the National Crowdfunding Association of Canada (www.ncfacanada.org). In the UK there is the Peer-to-Peer Finance Association (www.p2pfinanceassociation. org.uk), whose founding members are www.fundingcircle.com, www.zopa. com and www.ratesetter.com. There is also now the UK Crowdfunding Association (www.ukcfa.org.uk). It is interesting that www.seedrs.com, www.crowdcube.com and www.crowdbnk.com have joined the UK Business Angels Association (www.ukbusinessangelsassociation.org.uk).

If you are planning to set up a platform you should make sure that these associations know about you and that you know about them – it may well be worth joining one or more of them to benefit from the expertise of the people this will put you in touch with.

Other ways to make money out of the crowd funding revolution

Not everyone wants to or would be able to set up a crowd funding platform, but there are other ways to make money by serving this market.

White label sites

One way is to white label someone else's site. White labelling is when you license the technology that operates a platform and brand it with your own name. People who use your site probably will not know that you have not built the technology yourself unless you tell them. If you have a large crowd yourself – either of people needing money or of people wanting to invest it – this might be a very useful route to follow, especially if you are in a niche where the operator cannot get access.

Acting as an agent for a platform

If you have a good network of entrepreneurs and/or people who have money, or if you are a bit of a thought leader with thousands of followers on Twitter, it may well be worth you cutting some deals with various platform operators to drive business towards them. With the online world being so transparent you should be able to set up a system that ensures the introductions you make are properly tracked; then you can earn fees and commissions on the business you generate for the platform.

It is unlikely that you will get paid anything upfront, but the rewards can vary from being given an iPad or bottle of champagne (from MarketInvoice) to percentage commissions based on funds raised (from sites such as Crowdcube and Platform Black). Remember that 1% of a £100,000 fundraise would be £1,000 in your back pocket just for making a phone call or sending an email.

If you think that this type of arrangement would suit you, contact the platform operator (or operators) that you think your network will use the most and strike a deal with them.

It is worth noting, however, that if you are going to act as an agent, you have to keep working at it, so you will need a marketing and activity plan to ensure that you continue to drive your own income upwards. You will also need to monitor the clients you introduce to the platform to make sure that you get the rewards you deserve when the campaign completes successfully.

And, of course, you have to factor into your personal cash flow that typically you will not get paid anything until sometime after a campaign has successfully closed!

Acting as a specialist adviser on various aspects of a campaign

There is already an obvious role for experts in the crowd in areas such as video or business plan creation for campaigners. Many platforms already have a list of businesses and people they recommend you should use. A good example can be found at www.crowdcube.com/pg/investmentready-35.

With over 50% of campaigns still failing to achieve their targets, I suspect that over the next couple of years there will be plenty of business to be done in advising either side of crowd funding transactions. You will see specialists popping up who do everything from help entrepreneurs get their crowd pitch just right to help investors distinguish which opportunities to back – especially in the area of equity funding.

These are the main areas where there is business to be won for advisers in the crowd:

- business plan advice, particularly www.bizplans.co.uk
- financial forecasting, e.g. Johnny Martin (www.johnnymartin.co.uk)
- video planning and production
- legal and IP advice, particularly Taylor Vinters (www.taylorvinters.co.uk) and Gill Jennings & Every (www.gje.co.uk)
- tax and regulatory advice, particularly Saffery Champness (www.saffery.com) and Crowe Clarke Whitehill (www.crowehorwath.net/uk), Smith & Williamson (www.smith.williamson.co.uk)
- PR
- social media marketing
- app development
- due diligence services for investors, e.g. CrowdCheck (www.crowdcheck.com) and Massolution (www.massolution.com).

If you already offer these services in the traditional financing world, it would be well worth looking at how what you do can be adapted to suit the crowd world – or you might just find yourself sitting on the side lines as more savvy individuals and organisations grab business that you think should be yours.

Providing a full service advisory offering

Anyone wanting to build a business in the crowd could do no better than to look to www.massolution.com as a role model that is rapidly building a complete advisory service with different divisions that service everyone in the crowd. You can see from the case study below the wide range of services Massolution offers.

> ## Case study
>
> *Massolution*
>
> *Massolution is a US-based website owned and operated by Crowdsourcing LLC and has set itself up to offer a full range of services to the crowd. These include helping platform operators to find projects for their platform, choosing which types of fundraising to offer and helping them to build their crowd and to grow. It also helps them build operational systems that will be successful at managing campaigns before, during and after they take place.*
>
> *For fundraising companies it helps with all types of fundraising issues including modelling the likely success of campaigns on different platforms. And for venture capitalists wanting to invest in crowd platforms it assists with due diligence and provides market research to help them make investment decisions. It also offers help to the management teams that the venture capitalists back.*

Conclusion

As you can see, there are plenty of opportunities to make money running a business in the crowd funding world. If you are going to set up in business you need to follow the same rules that apply to any other industry. Do your research, have USPs, build a team to support you, have a decent plan, look after the cash, build a product or service that everyone really wants and is better and/or different from the competition, and get your sales and marketing strategy right. Personally, I cannot wait to see who else makes money out of operating in the crowd funding industry in the future.

In summary

1. The crowd funding market is very competitive and there are new platforms opening all the time.
2. If you want to build a crowd funding platform you will have to differentiate yourself.
3. Building an exceptionally strong brand is vital – that starts with your website URL.
4. Operationally speaking, crowd funding is very technical so make sure you have a good chief technology officer or other IT expert close at hand if you are not a techie yourself.
5. There are lots of wrinkles such as regulation and insurance you need to think about.
6. You need to be amazingly good at social media and PR so you can build yourself big enough.
7. You will need to be, or to have, at least one "front man" who acts as the face of your platform.
8. You can make money by acting as an agent to an existing platform operator and you might even be able to run a white label version of their platform.
9. There are loads of opportunities to make money helping fundraisers and investors in the crowd – from providing professional services such as legal advice to helping with things like video production.
10. It may be worth thinking about how you could join up with other experts to offer a full service offering to the crowd – this could include providing advice to both platform owners and to fundraisers and investors.

Part Two

Raising money in the crowd

Chapter 5

What the crowd likes to fund

Understanding what the crowd likes to fund starts with which crowd you are thinking about. First there is your own crowd, then there are the crowds that like to fund with pledges, lending and investment. Each one has its own characteristics.

Your inside crowd

The ultimate inside crowd fundraising

Crowdcube

In what was surely the best possible example of the power of having a strong "inside crowd," in May 2013, the UK-based equity crowd funding platform Crowdcube raised £1.5 million in a self-run funding campaign on its own platform. The fundraising was initially opened to Crowdcube's existing shareholders, who between them invested £250,000 in just five hours. The fundraising was then opened to all the subscribers on the Crowdcube platform and the remaining £1.25m was raised in just three days. A total of 259 investors bought into the fundraising, which gave them a collective 21% stake in Crowdcube, valuing the business at roughly £7.1 million. It was a recognition of the faith the Crowdcube community places in the platform, which was authorised by the Financial Services Authority earlier in 2013 and which, since its inception in 2011, has helped 56 businesses to raise £9.6 million from over 37,000 registered investors. Crowdcube has said that the new money raised will help it with its plans to grow staff, increase its marketing efforts and to expand overseas. It has its sights on entering the US, Swedish and Brazilian markets now!

If you remember I suggested earlier in the book, that the minute you start thinking about undertaking a crowd funding exercise, you need to start gathering the details of people you know who might be interested in helping you to get your project or business to its next stage. You can calculate the size of what I call your inside crowd by adding up your email contacts, your LinkedIn contacts, your Facebook friends and other contacts you have on different social media sites. To have a chance of being successful with crowd funding, you will need hundreds if not thousands in your inside crowd. For a lucky few you will also be able to include the existing customers and/or fans of your business in your inside crowd. Crowd funding is amazingly successful for those who already have thousands of happy customers who will tend to know all about you and what you are doing. An excellent example of this is Escape the City, which raised investment from its lively subscribers to support the expansion of its online service helping city executives.

Case study

Escape the City

Escape the City started with three bored London city workers who wanted a viable and exciting change. Dom Jackson and Rob Symington wanted to create a website that helped similarly bored professionals get out of the city and undertake adventures and exciting short-term projects. Since they were all about leaving the city, they were reluctant to receive city funding – despite two offers from venture capitalist funds. They went to Crowdcube in June 2012 and within nine days had raised £500,000. They then increased their target by £100,000, raising this extra amount in just four days. They have over 65,000 people signed up to their website, which helps with career transitions. Their plans for the money are to create an aspirational alternative to standard profiles such as LinkedIn, as they want to focus on the networking aspect of the site. They offered 24% of their company in equity to the 394 investors who helped them reach their £600,000 target in just 13 days. They managed to get the word out about their project by simply emailing their friends to ask for help and the response was phenomenal – and had the desired effect of the email being passed to friends of friends who were all bored in their city jobs – they were soon registering opportunities around the world.

As crowd funding is all about engagement, when it comes to your own crowd, think about what you can do to encourage them to back you. In fact, why not ask them before you start your crowd funding exercise about what they want to back and how they want to back you? First you need to get yourself organised so you can prepare an explanation of what you are planning to do; then you could send them a simple survey using an online system such as www.surveymonkey.com to find out what they think. Some of the questions you could ask include the following.

- Which of these projects would you back and why?
- What feedback would you like to get at each stage?
- Would you prefer to back me with a pledge or for a reward, lend me the money or invest in my company?
- Would you like your money back and do you want to make a return on the money?
- If so, what sort of return would you like to get?
- When would you like to get your money back?
- What would you want me to achieve with your money?
- What do you think I need to do before I ask you for money?
- What would you like to know about how things are going after you have given me your money?

Finding out these things will help you decide which crowd platform you should use and what offer to make.

When it comes to your inside crowd, you still need to be fully prepared with your offer before you reach out to them. And make sure that your offer is incentivised to reflect your relationship with them. For example, if you are going to approach the people who use your products or services, perhaps you need to offer them a generous discount or even free use of them for a while. This reward should be even better than the rewards offered to strangers.

The outside crowd

There are really two types of crowd funders outside your own circle; those who are happy to be identified and those who prefer to remain anonymous. Of course, some funders like to be identifiable on some sites and anonymous on others. The former can be found on pledge sites such as Kickstarter and on equity sites such as Crowdcube and Seedrs. They have to reveal who they are in order to get the rewards or shares you are offering. The latter are typically on lending sites such as MarketInvoice, Funding Circle and ThinCats, which do not reveal to the borrower who is lending them the money.

Case study

Eurojet Aviation Ltd

Eurojet was established in 1991 and specialises in providing bespoke private jet management and charter solutions to a wide range of clients including celebrities and high net worth individuals. Their new service and operations centre was opened at Birmingham Airport in 2012, although they also have bases at London and Belfast. With award-winning safety standards and a highly experienced team, Eurojet was a strong prospect for investment. Eurojet was seeking the loan to replenish its cash reserves following capital expenditure on the move to its new Eurojet Business Aviation Centre. Cessna also provided a £300,000 deferred purchase arrangement for spare parts to aid Eurojet with its move to the new premises, and the company wished to pay this off in order to move the relationship forward. Eurojet was ideally seeking funding of £750,000. This was achieved using ThinCats in two loans of £450,000 and £300,000 in December 2012, which took only six days to be fully funded. ThinCats' willingness to lend was vital to this growing business.

The common thread, though, is that these people do not know you and may know nothing about you or your business until the day you announce your fundraising. So it is essential that you are well prepared when they do come across you. The first step you have to take is to make sure that the public profile on you and your company is consistent, comprehensive and honest so it creates an immediate sense of trust. In particular, review what people can find out about you online and with a few phone calls. So check out your Twitter history, your photos on Facebook and your LinkedIn profile; Google yourself and find out what is up on the web. Remember that some information on you will be very public and some will be more hidden, so do some digging. Make sure you correct any errors and remove those embarrassing photos taken of you when you were younger! And lastly, it may also be worth finding some trusted referees whom people can call to find out more about you. Some of them may even be willing to write a testimonial about you (and post it on LinkedIn), which may be helpful.

Outside funders will be looking for you to meet the promises you make in your fundraising, so make them offers that will be directly attractive to them. When it comes to rewards, offer something you know they will like but which is also a bit special or even unusual – perhaps a personally signed copy of a book or a product with an enhanced feature. Remember that during the fundraising you will be able to judge this much better when you see which rewards people take up – you can then revise the rewards accordingly. If your fundraising has a social mission, make sure that you clearly outline the social benefits their money will provide.

For both equity and debt fundraising, you need to think about returns, i.e. the additional money you will pay to your funders over and above what they have given you. Even though the Bank of England base rate is at 0.5%, don't think that by using the crowd to borrow, you will suddenly be able to borrow at a very low rate of interest. In the debt funding crowd you are likely to find that interest rates are at least as high as those a bank would charge and may even be higher. This is because any lending to a smaller company is very high-risk. On many debt sites it is normally the lenders who set the interest rate, not you, but you can assume that you will be paying a rate that is in the mid teens. So make sure your business plan and cash flow projections show not only that you will be able to make the repayments, but also how you will generate the money to pay them.

When it comes to equity fundraising, the most important thing to think about is the valuation you are putting on your company today and what valuation you hope to achieve when you sell the business. This will affect what price you sell the shares for. Make sure you don't value the business so low that investors will think something is wrong, but equally don't get greedy and assume that because you are raising smallish amounts from lots of investors you can get away with overvaluing it. It is well worth taking advice from an expert such as an accountant or corporate financier and listening to the hints the platform provider gives you, as private and angel investors using crowd platforms are likely to be very savvy when it comes to valuation. Take a long hard look at other companies that are fundraising on the various platforms (not just the platform you have chosen) to get further guidance on how you should price your own shares. And it is worth remembering that many investors are looking for at least a tenfold return on their investment (regardless of tax breaks), so consider whether, if they buy your shares at £1 today, you will be able to return £10 for each share in a few years' time. And if you can, will this leave enough money from the overall sale to give you the returns you want?

Timing

When it comes to the crowd, timing is everything. First and foremost you need to make sure that you give the time to the campaign when it is running — from what people say, that means pretty much 24/7 throughout the life of the campaign. Secondly, you need to think about what timing will suit the funders. Don't make the mistake of starting a 30-day campaign in the UK in mid-December, for example, as virtually everyone will be a) tired at the end of the year and b) just about to take a holiday for 10 days over Christmas. Think about other wrinkles in the diary, such as the end of the tax year in the UK; timing an equity funding offering tax breaks such as those from the Seed Enterprise Investment Scheme (SEIS) or EIS so that it straddles 6th April is foolish. It would be much better to plan to end the funding in mid-March so that you pick up investors with some tax break cash to spare, so they can record it in the current tax year rather than the next one.

Making the campaign itself extra attractive

Whatever the platform, any campaign should give as much relevant information as possible to potential funders, both at the start and as the campaign progresses. Before you begin, have a good look at the format of how the information you provide will be displayed on the platform. Think about each section and what it needs to contain. Write it all up and get it perfect before you submit the information on the website. Start with a catchy strapline for your campaign and move on from there.

Case study

Blenders Eyewear

Blenders Eyewear's goal is to help put students through school while decking them out in affordable and stylish eyewear. Through their Blenders Scholarship Program, they help put college students through school while highlighting and fuelling the efforts of America's best and brightest young people. They aimed to start small, buying books and whatever they could, and grow from there alongside the students they support. Eventually, they aim to award substantial scholarships to students all over the US. By selecting candidates who are actively pursuing goals such as starting their own businesses, travelling the world and instigating community growth projects, they hope to both bolster them in their efforts and inspire their classmates. Their campaign on IndieGoGo, which ended in May 2012, had a target of $5,000 to kick-start their efforts through donations that bought

> *rewards, from a pair of their sunglasses, shout-outs on their Facebook page and posters, all the way up to private surfing lessons. Donations were received from 189 people, raising a total of $7,095, which connected them with their fans and built strong relationships with them.*

You should think about how the content looks when it is displayed. Make good use of short paragraphs, bullet points, web links and images to tell your story well. Make sure that the type of language you use will be understood by the funders, but also that it reflects the nature of what you are doing. So don't get all technical if your audience is going to be the general public and don't use too much slang just because you are a dude in the music industry. Never use profane language.

Remember that a picture speaks a thousand words, so in addition to your video (see below) think about how you can use images and photos to make your campaign more interesting.

You must also make sure that all the relevant information on your campaign is already available when you launch and that you update it as you get hold of new information throughout the period. This means ensuring that all background information is available – business plan, financial projections, copies of patent and other IP documents, etc. You also need to make sure that everything you put up is consistent and joined up. And pay special attention to the video – this is so important that here's a special section on it!

The video

Without doubt the thing that is most likely to "sell" your campaign to a funder will be your video. It is likely to be the first thing they look at and it replaces that crucial first face-to-face meeting that you would typically have in the traditional fundraising world. In Chapter 7 I will explain what the video needs to contain in terms of content, but these are the other things you should think about in terms of how it should look and feel in order to attract funders.

Remember that above all the video should reflect you and what you are trying to do.

- **Format:** Should your video be a film, a cartoon or a slide show with a voice-over?
- **Style:** Is it going to be relatively informal and friendly or very serious and hard-hitting? Think about how to make the style fit with your own branding and ethos, but also that of your industry. For example, if you are fundraising for a film, you will need to make a film-quality video. Remember that how you portray the opportunity will go a long way to creating a sense of trust among potential funders, so think about the tone in which you say things as well as what you say.
- **The voice on the video:** Are you going to be the voice on the video, or will it be the voices of your other investors, your customers, your partners and suppliers or others?
- **Length and pace:** How long will your video be? How will you break up the time in it to ensure you cover all the relevant points?
- **Content:** Is the video really a teaser to get the funders to look at all the other information you have provided, or is it aiming to do the whole sell in one go?
- **Professional or amateur production values:** If you want to create the video yourself, I recommend you keep it as simple as possible and probably opt for a slide show with a voice-over format.

Unless you are already very experienced in video production, I would suggest that you create a story board of what you want your video to contain, then, approach a professional video producer (even if that is a friend currently on a media studies course!) to create it for you. This may cost you around £1,000–£2,000 but it will be money well spent as great fundraisings always have great videos to headline their campaigns.

Staying awake during the campaign

When you read accounts of fundraisers, they all tell you about how time-consuming and stressful a campaign is. During the campaign period you need to be on your toes at all times. This is crucial because the attention span of potential funders will typically last only minutes, if not seconds. In particular, take these things into account.

1. **Keep monitoring the campaign:** You cannot watch your campaign 24 hours a day, but do set yourself a timetable for regular checks — perhaps three times a day for at least an hour. Use the time not only to assess how your campaign is going, including deciding whether you need to do more marketing to drum up interest, but also to look at other campaigns and see what they are doing better than you.

2. **Be proactive:** Make sure that you do everything you can to anticipate questions from potential funders. Provide updates regularly, not only on what you are doing but also on other things that are happening which might affect your opportunity. And make comments on announcements by other companies in your sector and on how they might affect your business or project.

3. **Be responsive:** When potential funders post a comment, reply as soon as possible, even if it is with a holding comment to say that you will go and find out an answer and get back to them. Give them a time for when you will come back with the information needed.

4. **Be prepared to move your position:** As your campaign progresses, watch for signs of particular interest. Maybe some rewards are more popular than others and you will need to extend them, or you may need to offer new ones. Perhaps you will see signs of particular interest from a certain type of funder (e.g. those based geographically close to you or those giving slightly larger sums of investment), in which case think about how you can encourage more of that type of funder to come forward.

5. **Be grateful:** Whatever else you do, make sure that you show how grateful you are for the support you are getting. Regular postings of "thank-you" messages will show the crowd what they are worth to you — this will help!

All of this activity will be noted by potential funders and will help turn interest into actual offers of funding.

The most attractive types of campaign

Although it is a truism, different types of fundraising attract different funders. Here are some guidelines to think about.

Debt funding

Debt funders are motivated to lend because they want to receive interest on the money they give you and get their original capital back at the end of the loan period. The level of interest they want will reflect the risk they are taking on you paying these sums over to them. It also reflects the interest rate they can get elsewhere.

The main reason for the explosive growth in the crowd lending market is that investors cannot get such good rates of interest from traditional sources such as banks and building societies. But that does not mean they are prepared to take stupid risks. Therefore, to make an opportunity attractive to a debt funder, you need to be able to show that you can repay your borrowings, so this type of fundraising is only suitable for companies that have enough cash after paying their usual business costs to make the interest and capital payments. Ordinary borrowing platforms such as Funding Circle and ThinCats are suitable for companies that are established and have predictable cash flows – and ideally those cash flows are relatively stable from month to month. They are most suitable for companies that need to fund a capital project that will enable them to grow. Alternative borrowing platforms such as those auctioning invoices (MarketInvoice and Platform Black, for example) are suitable for established companies with variable cash flows, as the loans are for only a short period and are against an invoice that will be paid on a certain date in the future.

The sectors and types of company that find it easier to fundraise on traditional lending platforms are:

- established companies with a longish trading record
- companies in asset-rich sectors such as manufacturing
- companies with strong positive cash flows, e.g. in IT
- companies with a turnover of over £250,000.

Case study

Homes Caring for Autism Ltd

Homes Caring for Autism (HCA) and its subsidiary Somerset HCA provide high-quality specialist care for autistic young adults with complex needs. Somerset HCA was set up in 2003, with HCA following in 2005. Richard Smith set up the first home in 2004 in order to provide more fulfilling care for young autistic adults, and HCA now provides nine homes in Somerset and Wiltshire. The aim was to enable residents to live well supported but semi-independent lives in a caring family environment. HCA has built up a very strong reputation based on the quality of its care, ethos and accommodation and has an inspirational director in Richard. He founded HCA with the following mission statement:

> "Each and every individual has the right to be treated as a human being. Individuals with autism have a right to be understood, a right to be listened to and a right to contribute to society."

HCA also recently started to provide supported living services for complex autistic individuals who live in their own accommodation. After the banking crisis, the major bank that provided loan facilities to HCA changed its valuation methods and demanded immediate capital repayments, as well as became unwilling to provide additional funding. HCA initially sought funding for a short-term bridging facility to provide additional liquidity in its 2011 loan. In May 2012, it was seeking finance to go towards a new home, which opened in December 2012. Its third loan covered the final payment to the developer of the new home. They turned to ThinCats, whose members lent £150,000 over two years in July 2011 and a further £200,000 over three years in May 2012. The third loan was concluded in February 2013, for £350,000 over four years.

Richard speaks very highly of the ThinCats service, saying:

> "We have completed two rounds of funding with ThinCats. With the first round, they were extremely thorough in visiting us and getting to know our business, therefore investing time in getting to know us. They helped us to put together a briefing document for potential investors. Our expectations with regard to timescales

and obtaining funding, at an acceptable interest rate, were comprehensibly met. As a result, when we wanted to look at further investment, we had no hesitation in approaching ThinCats again. The process was dealt with speedily and we were fully funded, with terms and conditions acceptable to us. Business has been growing at a compound 30% per annum and, given the banks' reluctance in this current economic climate to lend money, the support of ThinCats has been critical to this growth."

In this case, ThinCats was able to replace the bank's loan with the new lending and provided a rapid process from auction to disbursement.

The sectors and types of companies that will find it easier on alternative lending platforms are:

- companies with cash tied up in capital assets
- companies with A grade customer bases (such as FTSE100 companies and similar well established high quality businesses) who raise invoices on relatively long payment terms
- companies in sectors where they supply top-tier companies, e.g. professional services and human resources (HR) services.

Case study

Cable and Cotton

Back in 2007, Bryn Jones was unhappy with his then job when he travelled to Thailand and saw a new product that he thought would do well in the UK, thanks to its affordable luxury. The product was a new type of lighting involving a string of lights in different varieties of colours. He imported 36,000 of them from the supplier in China and Cable and Cotton was born. After a great response at trade shows, Bryn opened his first shop and the company grew 100% in its first year. Wanting to grow the company quickly to ensure he was the first to get his product to market, Bryn made an equity sale which resulted in another growth of 100%. He then applied for a traditional loan, but after three months there was still no interest from traditional lenders. Bryn needed the money to get stock to meet his plans for the next year, so he turned to Funding Circle for an easy way to raise the money he needed. Three weeks after applying for a loan of £50,000, more than 300 investors had helped him raise the money he needed. Bryn is now growing his business not only in the UK, but also abroad after successful online expansion into Scandinavia.

Equity funding

Even though equity investors have a high appetite for risk, there are some sectors that are always more popular than others. And some sectors remain almost impossible to fund even in the crowd. These include areas such as biotechnology and very heavy manufacturing businesses, which need millions of pounds in funding before they make any sales.

Partly because of the roots of equity crowd funding in pledge/reward crowd sites, equity funders love to fund companies in the creative sectors. This can range from social media to new products such as high-tech watches. They also love to fund sites where there is an easy-to-understand consumer proposition, especially, it appears, in food and drink!

Case study

Financial Fairy Tales

Daniel Britton has combined his experience from previous careers in banking, teaching and education consultancy to produce innovative books and multimedia materials that are designed to help children learn essential money values, habits and principles. It was during his time as a teacher that he recognised a general lack of financial education and understanding in the education system. He then became an education consultant, writer and speaker on money matters before setting up Financial Fairy Tales in 2012 and developing a series of children's books that have already sold thousands of copies worldwide. After just five days on Crowdcube, Financial Fairy Tales secured £20,000 of funding from 22 funders in exchange for a 20% equity stake. Daniel used the funds to develop the products and market them. He commented: "I liked the control that crowd funding gives to a small business with solid potential like ours." There are currently three books on sale – Dreams Can Come True, The Magic Magpie *and* The Last Gold Coin *– along with an activity book full of games and puzzles to help children develop a greater understanding of the issues in the books.*

Other types of funding

If your funding need is not suitable for debt or equity, the chances are that it will be suitable for a donation or reward-based campaign. Everything from donations for scientific research and charitable projects to rewards for creative projects such as CDs, films or concerts can find a crowd platform that is suitable for them.

Case study

The Sum of Loss

When student filmmaker Toby Wosskow wanted to make a film of the "most beautiful script" he had ever read, he turned to donation-based crowd funding platform IndieGoGo. For a mere $50 he offered a copy of the DVD along with special thanks in the credits; for $100 you received the DVD, thanks and a signed poster – which would be valuable when he became famous! Donors who gave $500 got an associate producer title, and $1,000 promoted the donor to executive producer status. A total of 38 funders came together to help Toby make the film The Sum of Loss *a reality – it's a dramatic film that follows a distraught father who undergoes two life-changing events at once, making the audience question the presence of fate in their own life. With the majority of donors opting for the signed poster, he exceeded his $7,000 target and raised $9,621 to fund the project.*

The key thing to think about is what the reward will be. On donation sites, the reward comes from the wider good to which the donor is contributing. So you need to make sure you explain clearly what that wider good will be. When it comes to rewards, you need to tailor the reward to the amount of funds being given. Sites such as Kickstarter lets campaigners offer everything from token acknowledgements for donations of $1 to massive rewards worth several thousand dollars. When it comes to these rewards, you must make sure you build into your costs not only how much money it will take to get your project up and running but also how much it will take you to make and, importantly, deliver the rewards to your funders. Don't risk having all your funders come from a country far away, where the costs of delivering the reward via DHL will be prohibitive!

Case study

The Big Om

It's not just ordinary folk who use crowd funding as a method to get their projects off the ground. Stephen Russell, aka the Barefoot Doctor, used platform Sponsume to get funding for his live arena tour starting at Wembley in London on 12th December 2012. His idea is "The Big Om" – a project he describes as

> *"a vision of thousands of people celebrating human evolution, chanting the sacred sound of the universe – the OM – together and causing such a powerful vibration, the whole world feels it as an undeniable blast of healing, all backed up in a spectacular display of light and sound by state of the art electronic dance music."*

He offered backers the chance to buy tickets in advance, and for major donors the chance to meet the cast at the after-party. He exceeded his target and raised a total of £16,167 from just 214 backers. His supporters helped him by spreading the word: the link to his page was shared 1,046 times on Twitter, 1,828 times on Facebook and 200 times via email, and 2,870 copies of the link were posted elsewhere. Not only was this project funded by the crowd, but it was also marketed by the crowd.

Conclusion

Making a campaign fundable is therefore not just about what you do, it's about finding the right people to fund you, making the campaign as attractive as possible and choosing the right type of funding for your own circumstances.

In summary

1. There are two types of crowd – your own inside crowd and the outside crowd.
2. Your inside crowd includes everyone from your friends and family to your customers and suppliers.
3. Start building up your own inside crowd immediately – collect all their contact details, especially email, Twitter and similar ways you can reach out to them online.
4. Prepare your own crowd steadily in advance of your fundraising by staying in touch with them and telling them what you are doing.
5. Your outside crowd is found via crowd platforms – you may or may not be able to find out exactly who they are depending on the type of platform you use.
6. Make sure that the platform you use has an outside crowd that is likely to want to fund your business.
7. With the exception of donation platforms, all funders need rewards – tailor the rewards in your campaign to suit both your inside crowd and your outside crowd.
8. Schedule your campaign to suit the times when both crowds are likely to be most receptive and tailor the contents to make sure that the crowds will get all the information they need.
9. Prepare the campaign period to suit you as well. You will need to devote 100% of your time and attention to it when it is live.
10. Make sure you choose the right type of platform for the fundraising you want to achieve.

Chapter 6

Is crowd funding right for you?

It is now possible for you to raise anything from £100 to well over £5m via crowd platforms. And you can raise all types of funding, from pledges through to equity. So you might say that crowd funding is suitable for just about anyone with a cash need, but there are reasons why crowd funding might not be suitable for your business or project. It is worth considering these reasons before you leap into a campaign.

Wrong sector

One day I hope we will see enough platforms with different specialities to enable any type of business or project to raise money via the crowd, but at the moment crowd funding will not work for certain sectors. Ironically, those sectors are the very ones that will find it most tough to raise money from other sources. Good examples of tricky sectors include biotechnology and drug research.

When you are considering which platforms might be suitable for you, it is worth checking whether they permit your business or project to raise money at all, as the restrictions can be quite surprising. On Kickstarter, for example, you can raise funding for projects in these areas: music, film, art, technology, design, food, publishing and other creative fields. However, the following sectors (a lengthy list) are forbidden:

- alcohol (prohibited as a reward)
- automotive products
- baby products
- bath and beauty products
- contests (entry fees or prize money, for example within your project to encourage support)
- cosmetics
- coupons, discounts and cash value gift cards
- drugs, drug-like substances, drug paraphernalia, tobacco, etc.
- electronic surveillance equipment
- energy drinks
- exercise and fitness products
- eyewear (sunglasses, prescription glasses, etc.)
- financial incentives (ownership, share of profits, repayments, loans, etc.)
- firearms, weapons and knives
- health and personal care products
- heating and cooling products
- home improvement products
- infomercial or as-seen-on-TV-type products
- medical and safety-related products
- multilevel marketing and pyramid programmes
- nutritional supplements
- offensive material (hate speech, inappropriate content, etc.)
- pet supplies
- pornographic material
- projects endorsing or opposing a political candidate
- projects promoting or glorifying acts of violence
- projects using Kickstarter simply to sell existing inventory
- raffles, lotteries and sweepstakes
- real estate
- rewards in bulk quantities (more than 10 of an item)
- rewards not directly produced by the project or its creator (no offering things from the garage, repackaged existing products, weekends at a resort, etc.)
- self-help books, DVDs, CDs, etc.

(Source: www.kickstarter.com)

Other campaigns that are prohibited include:

- causes, such as charities, or a scholarship or 'fund my life' projects, such as tuition or bills
- equity or solicit loans
- reselling items not produced by the project/its creator
- those that promise to donate funds to a cause in the future
- e-commerce, business or social networking websites or apps

and last but not least:

- genetically modified organism can't be offered as a reward.

Make sure you check out your preferred platform to see if you are allowed to fundraise on it, before you face the embarrassing situation of finding your launch has been pulled.

Wrong type of funding need

In the crowd, there is not so much as a wrong funding need as a wrong place to tell people about it.

As far as I was aware at the time of writing, there were no sites offering suitable rescue finance to companies facing bankruptcy via the crowd, but pretty much every other type of funding can be found through the crowd, including funding for your own lifestyle projects (e.g. to go on holiday or pay for your education) through www.gofundme.com. There are loads of charity platforms such as www.justgiving.com as well. When you are considering what your fundraising need is, you need to think tactically, and use a site that matches your funding need in terms of:

- type of funding needed, e.g. reward, debt or equity
- size of funding, e.g. £1,000 or £1m
- type of project, e.g. creative, high-tech or consumer.

Remember that if you do not do your research and choose the right platform for your fundraising need, your campaign is very likely to fail, even if the amount of money you are looking for and all other factors (such as having a great product or a brilliant team) are right.

Wrong fundraising strategy

One of the interesting things about crowd funding is that while it is most attractive to start-ups which may see no alternative route to getting their businesses or projects off the ground, it carries risks – noticeably the bad publicity that may happen if the fundraising fails, the risk that the company loses some of its competitive edge by the competition finding out about it before it is ready to deal with competitive threats, and the risk that later investors may not be happy with it having been crowd funded originally. For really ambitious companies that are looking to raise business angel and/or venture capital finance when they are more established, crowd equity may even be dangerous, for similar reasons to start-ups.

Many angels and venture capitalists are extremely dubious (rightly or wrongly) about crowd equity, mainly because they envisage being asked to invest further down the line in a business that already has dozens or even hundreds of shareholders. At the moment, if they were presented with an opportunity which had a large shareholder base of small and possibly inexperienced investors, that would probably be sufficient grounds for them to turn it down immediately. That being said, it is interesting that www.seedrs.com is endeavouring to resolve this challenge by holding all their investors' shareholdings in a nominee account that acts as one shareholder in the case of decision making.

If you are thinking about raising equity from angels or venture capitalists in the future, it may be more appropriate to undertake pledge-based fundraising or a pre-sale of products or services, so that the money you raise does not have an impact on your shareholder register.

On the other hand, many businesses and projects are now undertaking successive fundraising rounds on some equity platforms – one good example is Kammerlings on Crowdcube (see page 19 for the case study). So, if you have the right type of business with a large crowd of followers that can only grow, maybe you should plan to do all your fundraisings via the crowd.

Another interesting trend we are beginning to see is where entrepreneurs raise money by more than one route. For example, they raise some money via angels and the rest from the crowd and other routes too.

Case study

The London Distillery Company (TLDC)

TLDC is a start-up boutique artisanal spirits' manufacturer at the forefront of the craft distilling movement in the UK. Its reason for fundraising was the production of a London single malt whisky – the first in over 100 years. The company also aimed to produce the only UK in-house organic London dry gin and a range of premium ready-to-drink barrel-aged cocktails. The founder, Darren Rook, had a background in bar and retail management and sales. It raised £250,000 with £150,000 coming from the Envestors angel network and the final £100,000 from the crowd on Crowdcube in 45 days. They also raised £100,000 of asset finance from Lombard.

Wrong stage of research and development (R&D)

IP covers things such as patents, trademarks, design rights, copyright, trade secrets and more. Many of these have to be registered properly to ensure that they are yours and stay yours. If you have a business that depends on its brand, or is making anything unique or even something familiar that is made in a unique way, you will have some IP that you, in theory, own. However, with things such as patents, trademarks and design rights, you own them only if they are properly registered with you. If their details get out into the public domain before you register them, the chances are that even if you invented them you will not actually own them. Other people will be able to use them without paying you anything and there will probably be nothing you can do about it. Therefore, it is *extremely* important that you tie up all your IP properly before you go public in the crowd. I would always recommend you talk to a specialist, known as a patent attorney, about this as soon as possible and definitely before you start fundraising, because the very nature of crowd funding means that the entire world can find out all about your business or project whether or not they decide to invest in it.

If your IP is not fully registered in your name and if you fundraise via the crowd, as well as risking other people stealing your ideas, you may also face serious legal issues. These can include the need to litigate against people who you believe have stolen your ideas, or, worse still, finding yourself in a litigation dispute brought by a bigger, richer third party who takes action in order to prevent you threatening their business because they believe you have stolen theirs.

Wrong amount of money, or the wrong platform for the right amount of money

On the face of it, there is no wrong amount of money to raise from the crowd, just as there is no wrong platform to use. There are platforms that can help you raise £1,000 and those that can raise £10m, but when it comes to money nothing is that simple.

Obviously, you are not going to try to raise £10m from a platform that has only ever raised £20,000 at the most for someone else, but what you really need to think about is what a platform typically raises for a business or project like yours. Kickstarter may have helped Pebble raise $10.5m but most projects on the platform raise $10,000 or less.

By August 2013, Kickstarter had successfully funded 46,358 projects, of which:

- 5,224 raised less than $1,000
- 30,131 raised $1,000 to $9,999
- 5,929 raised $10,000 to $19,999
- 4,316 raised $20,000 to $99,999
- 717 raised $100,000 to $999,999
- 41 raised more than $1m.

However, since its launch, 47,104 projects on Kickstarter have failed to raise the funding they wanted. Of these:

- 10,994 raised nothing
- 37,133 raised between 1% and 20% of what they wanted
- 7,091 raised 21%–40% of what they wanted

- 2,602 raised 41%–60% of what they wanted
- 841 raised 61%–80% of what they wanted
- 376 raised 81%–99% of what they wanted.

In the UK so far, only one company other than Crowdcube itself has raised £1m on a crowd equity site – the Rushmore Group in November 2011 on Crowdcube, even though the platform has raised between £100,000 and £200,000 for several companies since its launch. So the first thing to think about is whether the platform you want to use has a high chance of raising the amount of money you need.

The next thing to think about when it comes to money is how many people you will need to invest differing amounts to ensure that you get all the money you will need. This is where it all gets a bit tricky. You need to examine each of your chosen platforms to see what amount of money the most number of people will donate or invest. The answers may be more surprising than you think. On Crowdcube, the minimum amount which can be invested is £10 and the maximum anyone has invested to date is £100,000, but the average amount is £2,547. That is the average, though, and does not mean that most people invest this amount.

This is what Luke Lang, one of the founders of Crowdcube, had to say to me on the subject.

> *"Democratising investment to allow more people to invest smaller sums of money into start-up and early stage businesses is one of the underpinning philosophies behind crowd funding. Indeed, setting the minimum investment amount to be £10 was designed to be a clear statement of our intent to attract a new breed of equity investor. Since we launched in 2011, investments on Crowdcube have ranged from the £10 minimum to £100,000, with the average investment amount being £2,547 in a successfully funded pitch. Although under £100 investment amounts remain very common for backers seeking to 'support' a business or entrepreneur, the top end of the funding range demonstrates that 'traditional business angels' are also investing, which increases the average substantially.*

"It is still early days, but we are seeing a clear trend for 80% of the total funding target to come from 20% of investors.

"It's a really fascinating time for 'angel investment' – each day we learn more about the motives, behaviour and dynamics of crowd investing, which will inform platform improvements."

You should also think about other ways to raise money. For example, if you need to raise more than £1m equity, at the moment, but hopefully not for long, it is highly unlikely that crowd funding is the route you should follow. Instead look at angel networks and early stage venture capitalists to meet your needs.

Wrong amount of equity, interest or reward to give away

Raising money is not just about the actual cash you raise; it is about what you pay to get that money, either now or in the future.

When it comes to equity, you need to think hard about the value of the shares you are selling. On Crowdcube, the average equity sold by a business is 16%, but on other platforms it will be different. You need to do your research and see what amounts of equity other people have sold for their money in businesses that are similar to yours. It is definitely worth taking advice from a professional who is used to fundraising for companies on what the valuation of your shares should be. Remember that investors have a lot of choice about whose shares to buy, and you need to know the valuation of companies using angel networks and venture capitalists to raise money so that you do not over- or under-estimate what your own shares are worth. I will talk a little bit more about how you value your equity in the next chapter.

For debt, you need to think about the interest rate you will pay and the term of your loan. Interest rates can appear cheap or expensive at different stages in the life of a loan. Make sure that, if you are doing a debt fundraising, your cash flows can support paying the interest and the capital back in line with the schedule you agree.

Many pledge fundraisers have been caught out by the real costs of the rewards they promised so glibly months before in their campaign. When you are working out your rewards, make sure you fully account for the likely cost of delivering them to your funders and add this to all the other costs you will have in order to calculate the total amount you will need. A useful tip is to always add in an extra 10% contingency on top of that total amount at the very end of the calculation to allow for errors and unexpected expenses.

Remember: for every type of fundraising, you will have to pay the platform operator and the payment processor their fees too.

Once you have worked out what the fundraising will really cost you, you can decide whether the crowd funding route you have chosen will actually be able to do the job you need it to do. And your funders will pay you much more respect (i.e. are likely to fund you more) if they can see that you have done this exercise properly.

Wrong timing

I have already mentioned timing issues in earlier chapters, but it is worth stressing the things you need to think about again.

- You need to have all your ducks in a row before you start your campaign. If you are not ready, the chances are your campaign will fail. Think about plan A, plan B and plan C before you go live so that you face fewer unexpected challenges during the fundraising period.
- Avoid major events in the calendar that will impact on your fundraising – avoid Christmas, Easter and other major religious festivals when the last thing your funders will be thinking about is backing you. Also think about things like the end of the tax year.
- Think about your own life events – will the most intense period of your campaign fall during the days you expect the birth of your first child?! During your campaign you will have to be thinking about nothing else, so make sure you plan accordingly.

- You need to think about the length of your campaign. For every campaigner who raises their money in less than a week, there will be dozens or even hundreds still waiting for their money at the end of their 30- or 60-day campaign. Short, intense campaigns, rather than longer ones, tend to be the most successful, but this is only true if you have your crowd ready and waiting and you have enough people in your crowd to fund you. It may well be worth waiting to launch your campaign until you have greater certainty that there will be enough interest from the crowd to fully fund it.

Wrong type of personality

Let's face it, any crowd funding is as much about you as a person as it is about the project or business. People tend to back people. If you are a really shy, retiring type who never wants to get out there and hang out with the crowd, it will probably be a mistake to try crowd funding. It will also be a mistake if you are too sensitive, as the crowd can be as cruel as it is kind, and many fundraisers speak of how bruising a campaign can be as the crowd says exactly what it thinks and feels. Equally, if you are completely shameless, remember that a campaign will feed your ego possibly to a point where there could be a disastrous result – in this case you fail to be paid any attention at all. I recommend that it is best to have a small team in place already when you start your campaign, so you can share the stress and joys with others on the journey. Even if you are the one fronting the campaign, have some people waiting in the wings (even if it's your mum!) who can support you on the way through.

In summary

1. Although crowd funding may seem suitable for everyone, in fact different cash needs will dictate a) whether it is right for you, and b) if it is, which platform will get you the best results.
2. You need to choose a platform that is successful at raising funds for businesses in your sector – some platforms ban fundraising in certain sectors.

3. You need to choose the right type of platform for your fundraising; for example, don't try to raise funds for a business on a donation platform.

4. Make sure your fundraising strategy fits with your business needs and with the type of strategies popular on the platform you are using, but also with the fundraising strategies you may need or want to use later on. Note: not all angels or venture capitalists are comfortable yet with crowd equity-funded companies!

5. All your IP should be properly protected before you start your campaign – if you fundraise before that you risk getting your ideas stolen or worse.

6. Choose a platform that is used to raising the amounts of money you need.

7. Get your reward offers right. For pledge funding the rewards need to be a real incentive for the funder. For equity this means getting the valuation of the shares you are selling right – you probably need to get advice on this. With debt-based platforms, you will probably find that the crowd tells you what interest rate it wants.

8. Remember: crowd funding is not free. You will pay between 2.5% and 5% in fees to the platform provider. You may also have to pay other costs regardless of whether your campaign is successful.

9. Timing your campaign is critical. Make sure you avoid major festivals such as Christmas and Ramadan. Don't do a campaign for a "Christmas" project in February!

10. Don't undertake a crowd funding campaign on your own if you can help it, and be prepared for the criticism as well as the praise. If you are really shy and sensitive, crowd funding may not be for you.

Chapter 7

How to persuade the crowd to invest in you

There are three phases to a crowd funding exercise: planning, preparation and the campaign itself.

The planning phase

Before you start on a crowd funding exercise, it is vital that you understand various things.

You have to be willing to get very public about your business or project in the crowd world; this includes telling complete strangers all about what you are planning. You also need to accept that you may face questions on pretty much anything, from what you are planning to do to quite personal questions about yourself and other members of your team. This is particularly true if you are looking to borrow or raise equity. Therefore, it is vital that you and your business are well prepared for this scrutiny. Much of what you have to do to prepare for a campaign is similar to what you would do if you wanted to raise money from the bank, angels or venture capitalists, but when you are preparing you have to think about it all in the context of a very public and high-profile campaign, where you cannot afford to make mistakes unless you are ready to publicly admit to your errors once the campaign has started or (even worse!) once it is over.

These are the essential things to get right before your campaign starts.

Writing your business plan and executive summary

The business plan and the executive summary are vital to getting your crowd fundraising moving in the right direction. By writing a plan you can decide what sort of funding you need, why you need it and how you will use the funds you raise.

Give your business plan lots of attention – expect it to take a couple of weeks of solid effort in getting it right. Start with the business model you wish to follow and go from there – work out how you will deliver what you are planning. Think about what needs to be done first, then work out what resources you will need (including people), and finally build up a financial model for the business. Expect to redraft your plan several times as you develop your thinking. Write the executive summary last, once you are completely happy with your plan. Once it is written, get a couple of people you trust and who know about your business to read it through and give you comments.

Numerous books can be found on writing business plans. The ones that are particularly good are *The Best-Laid Business Plans: How to write them, how to pitch them* (Virgin Business Guides) by Sir Richard Branson and Paul Barrow, *How to Write a Business Plan* (with accompanying CD-ROM) by Mike McKeever, and *How to Write a Business Plan* (Creating Success series) by Brian Finch. You can also hire people to help write business plans, though you should remember that even if someone else helps you to write it, it is still your plan, not theirs – so you should make sure you are completely happy to take ownership over everything in it before you share it with anyone who wants to back you. One of the best sources of help is Business Plan Services (www.bizplans.co.uk).

Essentially, the business plan and executive summary need to include the following information.

- **The executive summary (remember: even though this comes first in the final document, you actually write it last!):** The executive summary is a two- to four-page document that has a paragraph or two describing each of the key parts of a business. It is a very important document, as it is probably the first thing the investors will see on your business and will also be the basis for the contents of things such as the video you issue during your fundraising. It should be a succinct summary of what is in your plan.

- **The business plan itself:** The business plan is one of the most important documents a company ever prepares. It is not a day-to-day plan of how you run your business, but is a document to attract investment. So, it is really a detailed advert for the company and it is the accepted method that entrepreneurs use to tell potential investors all about their business and why they need to raise money.

I have seen dozens and dozens of business plans in my life. Many of them are atrocious and may well have hidden a perfectly good business idea. It's a bit like the paper equivalent of the terrible pitches you see on TV shows such as *Dragons' Den*. The trouble is that a bad business plan will usually stop your fundraising in its tracks, whereas a well written plan will get you a long way towards successful fundraising.

The business plan is important for another reason. Don't be surprised when it comes to closing the investment if your investors ask you to sign a document confirming that everything in the plan is completely accurate as far as you are aware. It is therefore a good idea to get it right from the beginning.

Here is a list of key things to get right when you prepare your business plan.

- The main part of the plan should be 20–30 pages long.
- There should be attachments or appendices to the plan that include the management team's CVs, copies of the spreadsheets with your financial projections, customer references or orders, and information on any IP the company owns (e.g. patent details).
- Pay particular attention to the following sections of the plan: the business growth plan; competitor analysis; and use of the cash being raised.

- Beware of using jargon that everyone in your industry uses, but that investors may not understand.

The different parts of the plan that you need to include are discussed below.

Introduction

- What the company does, e.g. *We are a social networking website focused on students.*
- What stage it is at, e.g. *start-up, expanding, etc.*
- Where it and its customers are based, e.g. *The head office is in Leeds, UK and our customers are based in UK and US.*
- How it delivers its products or services, e.g. *The company operates via an online shop and we also have a mail-order catalogue that is sent out four times a year to everyone on our database.*
- What the competition is like, e.g. *The company has two major competitors, both of which are smaller in terms of sales and number of customers.*
- Describe the opportunity, e.g. *Following market research, the company has identified that it should start selling 25 new ranges online and open its first shop in central London.*
- How much money is being raised, e.g. *The company is seeking to raise £500,000 to fund the costs of expanding the range and to lease and fit out the premises for the new shop.*

Company background

- Number of staff and offices.
- The management team.
- Recent trading history, e.g. *The company has grown revenue and profits each year for the last three years.*
- The business model, e.g. *We are a virtual business. The company generates sales from thousands of consumers who pay online for their orders via their debit and credit cards. Goods are delivered via post within two to five working days, although customers can pay extra for delivery within 24 hours. We have a full refunds policy provided the goods are delivered unharmed. Our fulfilment is managed by XYZ plc, which also looks after ABC plc, DEF plc and GHI plc.*

- A description of the market in which the company operates, e.g. *We are part of the multi-billion pound online retail market which is currently growing at 10% a year.*
- What is different about the company compared with the competition, e.g. *We are the only business that has a website in 24 different languages.*
- Major achievements so far, e.g. *With only £5,000 of investment the company has generated £250,000 in sales and has customers in 24 countries around the world. No customer has ever claimed a refund! The company has won two major retailing awards in the last 12 months.*
- The immediate potential for the business, e.g. *We expect demand from customers to grow at 30% a year for the next two years.*

Future growth

This should describe the medium and long term growth prospects for the business and explain why you have come to this view, e.g. *75% of our customers have pre-ordered products from our 2008–09 catalogue even though the goods will not be available until summer 2008.*

Forecast

This section should have a table summarising the key financial numbers, including sales, profit before tax and net cash flows for the last two years (if you have been in business that long), the current year and three years into the future.

Do read Appendix IV, where financial guru Johnny Martin has written down everything you need to know about how to prepare your financial forecasts.

Funding requirement

- How much money will be raised?
- What will it be spent on?
- Your ideas of the value of the business.
- Any special terms to the deal, e.g. *The company wants to raise 50% of the money as a loan and 50% for shares. The company also qualifies for the SEIS or EIS for private investors.*
- Whether you intend to raise more money after this round.

Working out how much money you need to raise

One of the biggest problems crowd fundraisers find is that they do not raise enough money in their campaign to achieve what they have promised their funders.

This is the fool-proof way to work out how much money you should raise.

Work out your business costs on a monthly basis

Work out on a monthly spreadsheet what your various costs in each month will be over the next two years or so. Some costs will be the same or similar every month; others will be lumpier or even one-offs. Have a separate line in your spreadsheet for each of these costs. Start with the essential ones at the top and then list them in order of priority, with the least important at the bottom. These are the sorts of costs you should include:

- the essential costs you are going to have regardless of how big your business is going to get early on – rent, phones, travelling, PCs, software, etc.
- all your employment costs (especially employment taxes)
- the costs of things such as getting patent applications registered, getting your video made and any professional advice you will need to pay for, regardless of whether your campaign succeeds or not
- the cost of making and, importantly, delivering the rewards to your crowd funders
- the fixed costs you are going to incur to make and deliver your product or service to your customers
- the unit cost of your product or service and how many units you think you will want to make (remember that this may be larger than the number you want to sell, as you may want to have some reserve stock to sell in the future)
- what your contingency money should be – I usually suggest to entrepreneurs that on top of these costs they should assume a contingency of about 10% of their total costs each month, to allow for the following:
  - some things being more expensive than you think
  - sales not being as good as you hoped

- ○ unexpected costs you did not think about, e.g. unexpected travelling
- ○ wanting to spend extra on something you had not planned for.

Add up all your costs at the end of each month and then for the whole two years. This will give you your likely business costs over the period.

Work out your likely sales on a monthly basis

On a separate spreadsheet, but in the same workbook, set up a similar spreadsheet to list your monthly sales (both including and excluding sales taxes such as VAT).

You should first estimate the number of units of your product or service that you are going to sell each month. Then work out on a separate row what price you will sell them for. (Remember to take into account any plans you have to increase prices!)

On a new line multiply the number of units by the selling price for each month in your forecast. You will then have your likely income over the next two years.

Clearly, you may wish to turn this into a really extensive profit and loss and cash flow forecast. There are lots of good books and websites that can help you with this if that is what you want to do, and there is more information on this in Appendix IV.

Work out how much money you will need to get your project or business off the ground

Once you have all your sales and all your costs, you can work out how much cash you will need to keep going until you are making enough sales to cover all your costs. This will be the base amount of money you need to raise. However, you will need to take into account the costs of actually conducting the campaign before you can work out the total amount you need.

Work out what your fundraising costs will be

There are always real costs in raising the money you want. When it comes to crowd funding, these will include things such as:

- the costs you will incur making and delivering the rewards you are offering as part of your campaign (don't forget postage!)
- the fees the crowd platform charges
- any advisory fees you need to pay to lawyers, accountants, PR people, etc. to help you get your fundraising started
- fees for one-off items such as the video you make for your campaign
- miscellaneous costs, e.g. travelling to have a special meeting with a really big potential crowd investor who insists on meeting you in person or an unexpectedly large phone bill because you overspent on your contract during your campaign.

Remember that you will need to allow a margin of error when it comes to working out the costs of the fundraising. For example, the types of rewards you offer during a campaign might change a lot. Make sure you take this into account when working out your costs.

Finalising the amount you are looking for

Once you have got all your business sales and costs and the costs of fundraising, you should know roughly the amount of money you will need to raise. I suggest that you then round it up to the nearest whole unit that is sensible – so if your funding need is £9,400, set your fundraising total at £10,000. If it is £43,257, set it at £45,000 or even £50,000.

Getting your rewards offer right

One of the unique characteristics of crowd fundraising compared with other types of fundraising is that you can offer additional incentives to your funders to encourage them to back you.

Originally, the pledge funding model tended to use rewards based on pre-ordering of the product or service that the fundraiser was intending to sell in the future. Essentially, the fundraiser would offer to sell (effectively at a discounted price) one or more versions of the product, e.g. a film, book, DVD or song, with the promise that it would be delivered once it had been produced. However, with the explosion of the crowd funding concept has come an equally interesting explosion in the way fundraisers reward their crowd investors. Even in crowd equity, the most usual type of reward takes the form of one or more of the products or services being offered. Fundraisers may offer one product if you donate a small amount, but as you pledge or invest larger sums of money, you get more and more products or, alternatively, a more unique or specialised version of the product. With each type of reward, fundraisers can set limits; for example, only a limited number of people can pledge at a given amount. You will remember the earlier case study on the Pebble watch. Well, this is how it arranged its rewards.

Case study

Pebble e-paper watch

Pebble had the following rewards on offer in its mega-fundraising round in 2012. Although it originally intended to raise just $100,000, the interest in the campaign led to it increasing the rewards on offer repeatedly to keep up with the demand from funders.

- *$1: Keep up to date on all things Pebble with exclusive updates, Pebble availability or more. You can also sign up for more updates at http://eepurl.com/lG15L. 2,615 backers, not sold out.*
- *$99 or more: One jet black Pebble watch. This watch will retail for more than $150. Free shipping to USA. (Add $10 for shipping to Canada, $15 for international shipping.) 200 backers, sold out.*
- *$115 or more: One jet black Pebble watch. Free shipping to USA. (Add $10 for shipping to Canada, $15 for international shipping.) 40,799 backers, sold out.*
- *$125 or more: One Pebble in any colour (choose from Arctic white, cherry red, voter's choice or jet black). Free shipping to USA. (Add $10 for shipping to Canada, $15 for international shipping.) 14,350 backers, sold out.*
- *$220 or more: Two jet black Pebble watches. Free shipping to USA. (Add $10 for shipping to Canada, $15 for international shipping.) 3,800 backers, sold out.*

- *$235 or more: HACKER SPECIAL. You'll get early access to the SDK and we'll send you a prototype Pebble in August so you can get started coding. You will also receive another Pebble in any colour when the full batch ships. Free shipping to USA. (Add $20 for shipping to Canada, $30 for international shipping.) 100 backers, sold out.*

- *$240 or more: Two Pebbles in any colour (choose from Arctic white, cherry red, voter's choice or jet black). Free shipping to USA. (Add $10 for shipping to Canada, $15 for international shipping.) 4,925 backers, sold out.*

- *$550 or more: OFFICE PACK. Five Pebbles in any colour (choose from Arctic white, cherry red, voter's choice or jet black). Free shipping to USA. (Add $10 for shipping to Canada, $15 for international shipping.) 900 backers, sold out.*

- *$1,000 or more: DISTRIBUTOR PACK. Ten Pebbles in any colour (choose from Arctic white, cherry red, voter's choice or jet black). Free shipping to USA. (Add $10 for shipping to Canada, $15 for international shipping.) 482 backers, sold out.*

- *$1,250 or more: CUSTOM WATCH FACE. Let us create a custom watch face precisely to your specifications! Send us your ideas and we'll design a watch face just for you. You'll also receive five colour Pebble watches so you and your friends can share the fun. Free shipping to USA. (Add $10 for shipping to Canada, $15 for international shipping.) 20 backers, sold out.*

- *$10,000 or more: MEGA DISTRIBUTOR PACK. One hundred Pebbles in any colour (choose from Arctic white, cherry red, voter's choice or jet black). Free shipping to USA. (Add $10 for shipping to Canada, $15 for international shipping.) 31 backers, sold out.*

Note: at the start of the campaign Pebble stopped its rewards at the $1,250 level. Only when it became clear that the campaign was going amazingly well did they add the "mega distributor pack", but in doing so they raised an additional £310,000!

There are some important things to think about when it comes to setting the rewards in your campaign. The first thing to do is lots of research on what other businesses like yours have been offering as rewards. Then decide whether you broadly want to copy what they have done or do something very different.

Other things to think about are listed below.

What rewards should you offer?

You can see from the Pebble case study that essentially they offered Pebble watches to their funders. However, in my research I have discovered all sorts of rewards being offered – from the fairly mundane (a signed copy of a book, for example) to the more exclusive (e.g. an invite to a private viewing of a new show) and to the completely unusual and unrelated (e.g. the offer by one Kickstarter campaigner to write the name of the donor on the front wall of the fundraiser's house or another where the rewards included a string of hand-made sausages even though the fundraiser's project had nothing to do with food!). The message is as follows: do not think of what reward you have to offer, but think of the reward that the donor or investor most wants to receive and how they will value it. You definitely do not just have to offer some of your finished products as the incentive. In fact, for some campaigns it may be effective to make the reward very unusual, truly unique or even something really permanent – how about a plaque on the wall of your new office with the names of all your donors? If you put a lot of thought into the rewards your funders most want to receive, rather than those you feel you ought to give them, and set your imagination free, you are much more likely to come up with things that will really attract funders. Crucially, don't fall into the trap of offering what everyone else offers but bigger. That will be a ticket to failure.

How much will you charge for each type of reward?

It is essential that you charge enough for your reward to cover not only the costs of making and delivering it but also your set-up costs. If you do not "turn a significant profit" on each reward, you will not have enough money to run the business thereafter. You can see from the Pebble case study that broadly they were pricing each watch at around $100 and that even with the highest rewards you could not get a cheaper watch. This suggests that they had worked out that the unit cost of producing and delivering the watch was far less than $100. The Pebble case study also shows how the fundraisers had worked out that it would cost them extra to ship the watches outside the US, so they said upfront that if donors lived elsewhere they would have to pay more for shipping. This was a clever way of offsetting a cost that could otherwise have eaten up all the profits from the campaign.

How will you differentiate between the rewards you offer, depending on how much is pledged?

Pebble offered more and more exclusive rewards packages to those who donated larger sums, but interestingly, in the middle of the range of offers both the pricing and the type of reward was only marginally different. Small changes in the reward and the amount charged make a big difference, including something as simple as offering the donors greater (but limited) choice in the colour of the watch they would receive. As you can see from the case study, over 40,000 took up the $115 reward, but only 14,000 took up the $125 offer. And only 100 people took up the $235 offer.

What are the likely differences in terms of who takes up which reward?

It will be very hard to tell in advance which offers the crowd will find most attractive. Make sure you work out the different permutations of rewards and donors. Keep working on different permutations until you have three or four that will cost you broadly the same amount of money to fulfil and will still allow you to have surplus money to build your business, but that will allow you flexibility if your donors or investors opt for different types of rewards. When you are working all this out, include some offers that you keep in reserve to announce as extra incentives during your campaign.

You will then have to do a reverse check to see if the various rewards you are offering are actually worth the money from the donor's or investor's point of view. Above all, remember that the perfect reward in a crowd funding campaign is one that:

- costs you very little to produce and deliver
- is disproportionately highly valued by the donors/investors
- is something that means your donors will remember you, remain loyal and, most importantly of all both for your

campaign and in the long term, become real advocates for your business and encourage other people to back you and/ or buy your products and services.

A good case study that helps to illustrate this point is the one earlier in the book called *The Sum of Loss* (see page 99).

Valuing the opportunity

Funders will be looking for value and returns in any crowd funding situation. They will be balancing these expectations against the risks they will be taking by handing over money to you.

For equity funding, there are many ways to set the value of the shares you are selling. It is critical that you look at this hard; for example, you do not want to set the value so high that everyone thinks your shares are too expensive to buy, but neither do you want to set the price so low that you end up selling too much of your business (and risk losing control of it to your new investors). Remember that you can sweeten your equity in various ways. In the UK, for example, if you can obtain EIS or SEIS relief for your company, then UK tax-paying investors get generous tax breaks from the government if they invest in you. You can also offer investors indirect rewards in the same way that you offer rewards on project or donation platforms.

Valuing your equity - specifics

What a share in a business is worth on any one day to any one person is a topic that has generated screeds of research and is a subject of discussion across the financial services industry, among investors and among business owners on a general and specific basis every single day of the year.

However, even though there are lots of techniques to work out how to value your shares, in fact there are some very simple things to know and rules to follow. Here are the things you need to think about before, during and after your campaign.

- Your valuation is relative to other opportunities investors could invest in. Therefore, when you think about valuing your business, do your research and find out how much shares are being sold for in companies similar to your own.

- If you are a small, unquoted company, you are riskier from an investment perspective because it will be more difficult for investors to sell your shares. Therefore, your shares will be worth less than those of bigger, more successful companies, especially quoted ones where it is easy for investors to sell their shares. This means you need to discount the value of your shares against companies that are already big and successful. Normally a discount of around 30% is a good place to start.

- Small stakes in businesses are worth less than bigger ones. If a shareholder does not have a large enough stake to influence what goes on in the business, then it is worth less than one where the shareholder can influence change. Traditionally investors put a 30% discount on shares that do not offer control compared with those that have control.

- At different stages in an economic cycle the same shares will be worth more or less than at other times, depending on the sentiment of investors towards certain sectors and industries. When you are fundraising you need to think about what stage in the general economic cycle you are in. If the overall economy is weak, it will be harder for you to price your shares at a premium unless you have an exceptional story to tell. On the other hand, in a boom you are likely to be able to price your shares more highly.

- At the end of the day, valuation is a reflection of the money people make from an investment. This includes dividends they may receive before they sell and the price they are likely to sell for one day. If you can make the case that the value of the shares will grow exceptionally quickly post-investment and that an exit (and/or dividends) will be quick and achieve high returns, you can value your shares today more highly.

- There are many simple ways of valuing your shares. These include applying a multiple of current or future sales and/ or profits, valuing assets ranging from property to IP, and (though this is less used today and is clearly unsuitable for new businesses) looking at past performance and basing the valuation on that.

I really recommend you take advice on valuation from an expert who knows what they are talking about, such as a corporate finance adviser. But don't forget to ask them to explain what they are doing and how they have come to the valuation they give you. It also does not hurt to do some research of your own to act as a check and a balance against what they tell you.

Debt fundraising – specifics
When it comes to lending-based platforms, you need to think about what rate of interest you can afford and are prepared to pay for the money you are borrowing. You also need to think what the term of the loan should be (i.e. how long you will take to repay it).

Donation and project platforms – specifics
On project and donation-based platforms you need to value the rewards you are going to offer. When I spoke at Greenwich University about crowd funding in autumn 2012, a bright individual from the audience summed up the best way to think about this. He said you have to think about funders as falling into a bell-shaped curve. Very few people will give you either a tiny sum or a very large sum. Most will fund you within a broad band in the middle. The trick, therefore, to getting your rewards strategy right is to offer enough different types of rewards that you appeal to those in the middle band. For example, you might want to offer three different types of reward – one that appeals to the smaller funders, one for those with a bit more money, and an exclusive one for those who give you the most money.

What type of fundraising do you wish to achieve?
One of the joys of crowd funding is that you can raise the money you need by various routes – donation, rewards-based, borrowing and equity. And remember: you can add a social enterprise angle to almost any type of crowd funding campaign. So this is the first thing to think about once your plan is written. There are pros and cons to each type of fundraising and there are also some types of fundraising that are more suitable than others.

Let's consider the pros and cons of each type of fundraising.

Donation

+ You do not have to return anything to your donors, so it does not matter whether or not you succeed in what you are trying to do.
− Your funders are being truly altruistic, so you have to offer them something pretty special to get their interest.
− You will have a much more limited audience of funders.
− You may not have quite the same incentive to get on and deliver what you intend.

Case study

SUDS

SUDS – or Send Us Your Dirt from Sandy – is a crowd funding initiative set up after Hurricane Sandy hit the east coast of America on Monday 29th October 2012, which left many thousands of people affected by flood waters that brought sediment (mud, sand and dirt) into homes and businesses. The founders of the campaign were interested to see the effect on the environment this sediment had as it affected public water supplies and sewage treatment plants with chemicals such as arsenic. As well as asking for funding to help with the project, they also asked people to send in samples of dirt from their area for analysis. Donors would receive anything ranging from a thank-you email to a copy of the final report and a presentation of findings from the founders. The campaign ended on 28th January 2013, having raised $1,400 from 18 funders (the original goal was $910). They hope to identify areas that need further treatment and attention, as well as determining the extent of any contamination deposited as a result of flooding from Hurricane Sandy.

Rewards-based

+ You don't have to sell any equity so people cannot interfere in what you are doing.
+ You will have an engaged gang of supporters who will champion what you are doing and that should lead to lots

more ordinary sales of your product or service in the future as they recommend it to their friends and contacts.

+ Once you have delivered your rewards, you still own everything yourself.

− You have to deliver what you are promising. This is not a project, this is a job – which means you have to take it very seriously.

− There will be a real impact on your life – you will have to think about and deliver against a timetable, a budget and more.

− You may not be able to get the support you need when things get tough.

Case study

The Cosmonaut

The Cosmonaut *is one of the most successful creative crowd funding projects outside the US. The original science fiction film about two young friends who are training to be astronauts at the height of the Space Race in 1967 quickly turned from a short film with traditional financing to a full-length feature film funded by the crowd and released online for free under a creative commons licence. Inspired by earlier successful films,* The Cosmonaut *became the first Spanish film to raise finance through the crowd funding method. The producers created a three-part plan for the financing – allowing for private investment and sponsorship as well as crowd funding. Using the Spanish platform Lánzanos, they raised €121,000 over two years and received an additional €121,000 from a private investor. At the last minute, the investor pulled out and the Save The Cosmonaut campaign was launched, reaching €131,000 in just three days thanks to 600 supporters, which at the time beat all crowd funding records. This support from the audience made the film possible, showing the power of the crowd and the weakening dependence on traditional sources of funding for creative projects. The film trailer was released on 14th February 2013 with the full film available to watch from www.en.cosmonautexperience.com from 18th May 2013.*

Another good case study on how successful rewards-based campaigns can be is the one on *Veronica Mars*, which you will find in Chapter 12 (see page 196).

Borrowing - straight debt

+ You do not give away any ownership or day-to-day control of the business.
+ Provided you meet your interest and capital repayments, you will be left alone to get on with your life.
− Remember that if the borrowers take a legal charge on your assets, e.g. those in the business, this information may become a matter of public record, for example at Companies House.
− If you fail to make interest and capital repayments, the consequences can be severe. You may find that the borrowers end up owning your business and, if you have provided security, they may end up owning the underlying assets you pledged as well.
− Borrowing can be expensive and can be a real drain on cash in the future.
− You are promising to pay well into the future − and you cannot predict today how life will look then.
− Borrowers still take a healthy interest in how you are doing, even if they cannot interfere, and you will have to give them your time and attention to ensure that they do not start worrying unnecessarily.

Case study

Wifinity

Wifinity is the largest service provider of recreational internet for the Ministry of Defence. Currently, one in six soldiers in the British army use Wifinity. The company was formed five years ago, in August 2007, and provides wireless and wired internet services to all of the major garrisons across the UK and Germany. Wifinity also provides the same service to defence training establishments such as the Royal Military Academy Sandhurst, the Defence Academy and the Defence School of Transport. There, students have access to training resources via a virtual learning environment hosted through the wireless network. Expansion is driven by adding sites, as installed sites deliver highly profitable "annuities" and predictable profitable growth. Increasing the number of sites increases the annuity and, therefore, the value of the business. Further growth is looking likely, and part of the funding sought was to develop that potential. Banks were unwilling to lend to a projection-led opportunity and so Wifinity's team looked elsewhere for funding. Managing director Aubone Tennant says:

> *"Frustrated with the lack of commerciality of the banks, and not willing to dilute equity, we obtained assistance from Sterling Capital Reserve and ThinCats."*

Wifinity has received £650,000 so far from ThinCats' lenders. This is comprised of two loans: the first for £300,000 was concluded in November 2012 and the second for £350,000 in February 2013. The loans reached their target in incredible speed – the first loan was fully funded in two days, whereas the second took only a day!

Borrowing - alternative debt

+ As with ordinary borrowing, you do not give away any ownership of the business.
+ Provided you pay off the loan on time you will not incur any penalties.
+ The borrowing does not become public. For example, in invoice auctioning your customers will not know that you are borrowing against their invoice.
− Borrowing is expensive.
− You will certainly still be responsible for the debt and you are likely to be responsible for collecting any money owed that will be used to pay off the debt. For example, if you auction an invoice you will still be responsible for making sure that invoice is paid on time. And if it is not paid on time you will face additional charges from your lenders.
− Lenders will still take a healthy interest in how you are doing, even if they cannot interfere.

Case study

Connected Pictures

Connected Pictures is a London-based independent production company which creates cutting edge video and digital content for many different platforms. One of Connected Pictures' main challenges is that many of its large blue-chip clients, such as British Airways, will typically take 90–120 days to settle invoices. The company needed to find working capital to invest in growth, but didn't want to upset vital clients by aggressively chasing debts, nor reduce the value of its orders by offering early payment discounts. So it turned to MarketInvoice's invoice auction model. Under this system the company selects which customer invoices it wishes to raise finance against, with larger invoices being shared across several different investors. Connected Pictures is now regularly raising instant cash of up to 85% of its total invoice value. Fees are typically around 1.25% of this value and can be estimated using MarketInvoice's online auction calculator.

Equity

+ If you fail, your investors fail too, but you do not owe them anything.
+ You can get access to all sorts of non-financial support and advice from your investors.
+ Your investors are quite likely to understand when you go back to them with a request for more money.
− Having investors is a moral and legal responsibility. There is lots of work you will have to do to look after them over and above the day-to-day running of your business.
− You have to run your business (especially if you are a director) in the best interests of your investors as well as in those of the company, which may mean your options change in the future.
− If you go bust, people may ask questions. If you do something badly wrong there can be legal repercussions, such as being banned from being a director of another company or even being prosecuted by the authorities. If

you are found guilty of crimes such as fraud, you can go to prison.
- It is normally very difficult to get back the shares you have sold.
- You will be sharing the ultimate rewards when you sell the company with other people, so make sure that any eventual exit will give you enough money to make it all worthwhile.

Case study

The Rushmore Group

The Rushmore Group is the well established owner and operator of members' bars and clubs in London – Milk & Honey and The Player in Soho and Danger of Death on Brick Lane. It also owns bars in New York and The Clubhouse boutique hotel in Chamonix in the French Alps. It is an ambitious group that wanted to expand by acquiring, refurbishing and opening a new members-only club in Soho, London. After launching the campaign on Crowdcube, the group approached its 300 members as potential investors to help raise £1m – for just 10% equity. The incentives were based on existing members' needs, including a generous bar tab and a lifetime membership to the club. They also were granted tax relief due to the higher than normal amount of money raised, meaning that those who invested £5,000 were granted 30% EIS relief. By tailoring their incentives to their existing members, the group didn't need to worry about marketing its campaign as much as other projects do. It wanted to remain exclusive, and 143 investors helped the group reach its £1m target in just 32 days during November 2011. This case study shows the importance of tailoring your incentives to investors to make your proposition attractive.

Social enterprise
- + There will be a lot of feel-good factor about what you are doing.
- − Some of your options in the future may be limited as you will have to remain loyal to your social responsibilities and more widely to "doing no evil".

Case study

City Shine

City Shine wanted to employ the homeless to provide a premium shoe shining service, and they turned to Buzzbnk to get started. They chose shoe shining as it is a service that is well known and easy to teach, and includes lots of face time with customers. They were also hoping to deal directly with businesses wanting to offer a perk to their employees and visitors, as well as establishing the more traditional "pay per shine" stalls around cities, in stations and airports, and even at events such as trade shows and weddings. Their service planned to train motivated homeless people, and give them the tools and confidence to provide a competitive service. From there they would go on to support them in one of two choices: self-employment, offering flexibility and control for those who wanted it; and direct employment with the stability and security that provides. Incentives included a shoe shine tutorial video and even a capped return on their investments. They topped their initial target of £1,500, which would enable them to start their self-employment model, and reached a total of £2,790.

Choosing your platform

In Appendix III, you will find a list of major crowd funding platforms currently in operation in the western world. You will see that there are several sites in each category, and it is well worth researching each website to see how suitable it might be for you.

The key things to look out for are:

- the types of crowd funding that work on that site
- success rates for campaigns
- fees and other costs, especially whether costs differ on a platform depending on particular circumstances, e.g. if you raise a really considerable sum of money
- restrictions, such as whether the platform allows you to keep the money you raise even if you don't hit your target
- what information you need to supply as part of your fundraising

- what legal and regulatory requirements you must comply with before, during and after your campaign
- how you interact with funders during your campaign.

When you are doing your research, have a good look around the various LinkedIn groups focused on crowd funding. This will help you to understand which platforms are the most successful and which ones will be right for you. At the time of writing, some of the most active LinkedIn groups are:

- Crowdfunding and Crowdsourcing, with over 17,500 members
- Crowdsourcing and Crowdfunding, with just over 1,500 members
- Crowdfunding, with just under 1,500 members
- Crowdfunding USA, with over 600 members.

There is also a relatively new group on Google+ called Crowdfunding which is worth keeping an eye on.

Websites worth looking at include www.crowdsourcing.org and www.equitycrowdfundingdaily.com, which is an American site but will provide pointers: as crowd funding is most developed in the US, you can be fairly sure that where the US platforms lead, those in other countries will follow.

Another place to find the most up-to-date information is Twitter. In the first instance I suggest you start following the feeds of the various crowd funding companies and their co-founders as well as commentators on crowd funding. Don't worry too much, as the more active you get on Twitter the more people will follow you, so the information you need will start coming to you rather than you having to find it. And remember that your Twitter crowd will become very important to you once you start your campaign.

Should I use more than one platform simultaneously?

I would not recommend that you use more than one platform for a campaign. But for some people who have different fundraising needs it may be worth undertaking a debt funding on one platform and an equity campaign on another. As the market is developing so rapidly at the moment, it would be worth taking soundings from platform operators as to whether you should do this before you start a campaign.

Most platforms will not allow you to undertake more than one campaign at a time, so watch out for that one!

Timing

There are two issues around timing your fundraising. The first is choosing which time of year to launch your campaign and the second is how long it will take you to complete it.

Choosing when to launch a campaign will be a very personal decision. It will partly be based on when you are ready, but it's also worth working out when will be the optimal time to launch.

For equity fundraising, for example, especially if you are looking to capture a number of biggish investors, you should time your campaign for the peak fundraising periods of the year: January to March, April to early July, or mid-September to early December.

You should also think about how long the fundraising will take – don't forget that it will take time to get your fundraising approved on your preferred platform.

Times also vary enormously depending on the type of funding you are looking for. If you are auctioning invoices via MarketInvoice (www.marketinvoice.com), for example, you can typically expect to get your funds within 24–48 hours of putting your invoice up on the site. Some borrowing platforms such as ThinCats (www.thincats.com) are also seeing loans get funded in a couple of days. However, timings for project and equity funding can differ widely. Financial Fairy Tales raised the funds it wanted on Crowdcube (www.crowdcube.com) in just five days, but typically most equity platforms have fundraising periods of 30, 60 or 90 days.

Case study

Lancashire County Council

Lancashire County Council and Funding Circle announced the first local business lending partnership in November 2012 as a way to help small businesses in the region to find funding. The economic development arm of the council – Lancashire County Developments Ltd (LCDL) – is lending an initial £100,000 to the scheme; this will fund approximately 20% of the loan that businesses apply for. After going through Funding Circle's application process, the rest of the loan will be opened up to investors to help small regional businesses to grow. This trial is being used as a blueprint for the future of small business lending across the UK, and the pilot scheme will help realise the growth potential of local businesses that are currently being stifled by poor access to finance. It is anticipated that the partnership could grow to a multi-million-pound commitment over the next five years. The partnership will provide important support for businesses in the local area to expand and employ additional members of staff.

When it comes to planning the timetable, make sure that you have plenty of time available during the campaign so that you can be both proactive and reactive. If you are not using those platforms where the operator will only accept your funding proposal if they are pretty certain they will be able to fund it (for example, some of the alternative funding sites such as MarketInvoice), you will probably need to be very active in stimulating interest from funders throughout your campaign. You will also need to be available to react to comments and enquiries from funders interested in backing you, so make sure you free up your own diary to do this. If you already have a business that is up and running, you may need to plan to delegate day-to-day trading issues to someone else in your team. If you are a completely new start-up, you will need to allocate part of your time to your campaign and other time to keeping the plan on track.

Gathering your crowd

The worst-kept secret in the crowd funding world is that not all crowds are the same. Of all crowds, your own one will be the most important to you, as people tend to back people they know and trust as much as – if not more than – their idea.

Therefore, from the moment you start thinking about a crowd fundraising campaign, you should start gathering the electronic contact details of absolutely everyone you know, from friends and family to customers and suppliers, and even contacts such as former business colleagues, in preparation for letting them know about your campaign.

You should also start your strategies from day one on building your crowd in other ways. Get active on Twitter, Pinterest and Foursquare, join relevant LinkedIn groups and engage in conversations on them, and make sure your Facebook and LinkedIn profiles are up to date.

Gather all the contact details in one place – anything from an Excel spreadsheet to a contact management system – and religiously add to them every time you come across someone you think might be interested in your campaign when it goes live. In particular, work out who your biggest champions are likely to be and how much they will fund themselves or as a result of their actions. For them, and for every other person in your crowd, try to get into their mindset and work out what they will want from you and what they will fund.

Case study

Baba Brinkman – The Rap Guide to Evolution

Baba Brinkman has a master's degree in medieval and renaissance English literature and wrote his thesis on the parallels between literary poetry and hip-hop music. After graduating, he went on to perform rap shows such as The Rap Guide to Evolution *– a show that won the Scotsman Fringe First Award in Edinburgh in 2009 – and* The Rap Canterbury Tales. *With an existing following of 800 Twitter followers and 2,500 Facebook fans, Baba wanted to expand on his* Rap Guide to Evolution *CD and make it into an educational DVD with additional teaching materials. The DVD already had the financial backing of the Wellcome Trust through a grant submission, but the additional funding*

> from Crowdfunder enabled the production of original animation and digital effects and the licensing of high-quality nature footage from the BBC. During the 45 days that his campaign was active on Crowdfunder, Baba made sure that he frequently updated his pitch and spread the word to his followers. In the end, he exceeded his £10,000 target to reach £12,588 from over 300 people. A donation of over £1,000 could book a full performance of The Rap Guide to Evolution at the donor's local school or theatre during 2011. The Prince Charles Cinema in London was one of the organisations that obtained bookings this way, securing the DVD's red carpet premiere at their Leicester Square venue.

Plan B

Although everyone sets out on a campaign to succeed, it is a good idea to work out now what you will do if it fails. And remember that you may face real cash costs from conducting your campaign even if it fails (e.g. fees), so build a kitty for those, and for your living costs, so that your world does not collapse with your campaign.

There are no rules to say that you cannot seek funding from places other than the crowd during a campaign, so use this planning phase to consider traditional forms of finance such as bank lending and angel or venture capital funding. You may also want to take a look at areas such as grant funding.

Remember that angels and venture capitalists are now taking a particular interest in crowd campaigns on all types of platforms. They are keeping an eye out for the next big product or service success story that they can fund. Even campaigns that have failed on the likes of Kickstarter have still drawn interest from customers and even investors, as you can see from the case study below.

Case study

Spark

Spark is a hardware start-up that makes products for the connected home, starting with connected lights. It was founded by Zach Supalla, who used to work for Groupon, and in November 2012 commenced its first Kickstarter campaign. Some 30 days later, Zach and his team had to acknowledge that there was not enough interest to reach their $250,000 target – their 1,601 backers had pledged only just over $125,500. The campaign failed and "in a way it was as if it had never happened", Zach told people. But the team learned a lot. Spark launched its own pre-order site and had $20,000 of pre-orders booked within the first three hours of it going live. Within two days, Spark had sold half the total number of units that it sold in its entire Kickstarter campaign. And these are orders that the company has held onto. Spark and its products have received lots more publicity than they did before or during the campaign, and also considerable interest from business angel investors. Supalla attributes this interest from investors to his Kickstarter campaign. He explained how he met many of the business angels because they responded to his $10,000 partner-level offer, which said "Hey, big spender. Let's talk." By doing this the company gave a big signal that it wanted to talk to investors without actually trying to raise equity investment during the campaign. The company is now in discussions with several potential equity investors.

Preparation

Preparing for your fundraising will be one of the most exciting and challenging things you probably ever do. The trick to success is to prepare to the nth degree and also to put in place strategies so that you can move and adapt as you go along, as there will inevitably be surprises along the way.

Hopefully, now that you are at this phase, you will have a really strong business plan ready, and you will also have decided which type of fundraising you want to do and which platform you want to choose. Once you have done all this, these are the steps to follow.

Setting a specific timetable for your campaign

Do not expect the web to do your work for you. One of the major differences between a successful and an unsuccessful campaign is that the person managing the fundraising reacts and adapts during the campaign itself. Therefore, you and your team need to choose a time that really suits you. The sorts of thing to think about are not only major holidays but also things that will affect your personal timetable – such as your mother's birthday party!

Gathering the information you will need to support your campaign

Typically, the sorts of information you will need are:

- an executive summary
- a business plan
- the founders' CVs
- details of any IP, such as patent and trademark documentation
- financial forecasts
- samples of main customer and supplier contracts
- a video
- a website.

The video is key!

Of all these, probably the single most important thing to get right is the video, as this will be what your funders will look at first. Although some people do have successful campaigns with fairly (or totally) amateur videos, if you want to raise serious money you need to take the video very seriously. If you are not an expert in creating videos, I think you should definitely employ an expert to help you get this right, even if that costs you some money upfront. If your business is about something consumer-focused, and especially if you are raising money for something in the media or the visual arts, your whole project will be judged on the quality of your video.

If you base the content on your executive summary, you will not go wrong in terms of what it has to contain, but don't be tempted to make the video too "busy" or "wordy". The trick is to be succinct and make sure that the video reflects you, your business and the values you have. There is no point in making a jokey video, for example, if in fact you are a naturally serious person, as funders will find it inconsistent and then be suspicious of you.

Remember: a video does not actually have to be a video. It may be a film (with or without words and music), a cartoon or even just a snazzy slide show (using the presentation software Prezi (www.prezi.com) can be very effective).

Having said that, most investors do not actually base their investment decision on the video, so don't allow it to overtake everything else in terms of importance. Just make sure it is a really interesting summary of what you intend to do, who is going to be involved in the project and why you have the dream you have.

Your website and you personally on the web

It is easy to forget in the rush of a crowd funding campaign that funders will dig around to find out more about you on the web. So make sure that your website is updated and that it looks and feels consistent with your campaign. You should also make sure any Facebook pages or LinkedIn groups you manage are up to date (and kept up to date during the campaign) and you should update your and your colleagues' personal profiles on Twitter, Facebook and LinkedIn.

Getting the crowd ready for the campaign launch

By this stage you should have gathered a considerable list of your own potential funders. During the weeks running up to the campaign launch, make sure that you are talking regularly to these people, but don't reveal too early on that you will be launching a campaign. Instead, talk to them about how your plans for your business or project are getting on, and tell them about any exciting developments that happen. You can also talk to them about interesting events happening in your industry or about things like how the economy is affecting you and your business. Aim to tell them stuff that they will want to pass on to others, so don't make it all self-promotion – this will quickly be spotted and then discounted.

Try to talk to them at least once a week, if not a bit more often. Don't fall into the trap of talking to them every day for a week, then ignoring them for 10 days, only to blast them again for a few days. It is worth looking back at the case study on "The Big Om" in Chapter 5.

The campaign

Launch

Hopefully you are now ready for launch. You have cleared your diary, the campaign looks perfect, and the answers to anything and everything any funder could ever ask you will be accessible at the touch of a button.

So, what should you do now?

1. Keep running your business/project anyway – talk to suppliers, keep designing the product, composing the music and whatever else you need to do.
2. Get everything ready for the campaign – prepare your draft campaign on the platform and have your press release and first tweets and LinkedIn and Facebook posts ready. Brief privileged people such as important journalists and funders "under embargo".
3. Press the button and you are off!

During the campaign

1. Keep an eye on your campaign at least three times a day, especially on any blogs or boards relating to your campaign. Respond to queries as soon as possible (even if that is the middle of the night!) and definitely before you go to bed.
2. Try to stick to your marketing timetable, however difficult that gets.
3. Keep everything up to date – adding new comments and photos as events proceed.
4. Keep encouraging your crowd to spread the word.
5. If events take place that mean you have to rethink your campaign, e.g. the rewards you are offering or your

marketing campaign, get on with it as soon as possible. Hopefully you will have ideas in your Plan B documents.

6. Get on the phone to your key champions and ask for their support – make it easy for them by having tweets ready for them that they can just copy and paste.

7. Don't go mad with the PR – phase it to fit with your campaign. So have a big blast in the first two days of the campaign, then give it a rest. Make sure you are then tweeting and posting every two to three days to keep up the momentum both on the campaign platform and via Twitter and other sites, so you can keep current funders interested and bring more on board all the time. Make sure your tweets are at least two of the following:

    o positive about what you are doing
    o showing the progress you are making
    o relevant to the campaign
    o interesting to the audience (not just to you!)
    o amusing to the audience (not just to you!).

There will also be certain moments during the campaign when you will have to react in particular ways; these are discussed below.

The dull points

There will inevitably be points during the campaign when nothing seems to be happening. These quieter times should be used to check and double-check what you have done so far, to amend rewards and plan for the next busy phase. It's also the moment to go out and grab a couple of hours with your friends down the pub or catch a film or concert.

The crisis

Until you launch, you will not know what unexpected things will throw a spanner in the works. This includes, I promise you, being too successful and not being prepared for it!

It's the crises that sort the sheep from the goats in the crowd. How you react will be vital and the trick is not to panic. During a crisis, time can seem to disappear more quickly than at any other moment of your life, but in fact you always have more time than you think. Do not be panicked into reacting without thought and planning. Even during a crisis, you should aim to remain in control of the campaign and not let others take over from you. Even a hostile journalist will respect you more if you respond to a surprise call with a "can I think about it for 10/20 minutes and then call you back with a full comment" – just so long as you do call them back!

And if a crisis takes place that you cannot possibly control but which will impact on your campaign (e.g. a national disaster), prepare a relevant response to the disaster itself and look up your Plan B to see what you can do to either keep your campaign on the rails or shut it down temporarily.

The last week

Anticipate that the last week will be as intense as the first. If your campaign has clearly failed, this is the time to prepare the "thank you, anyway; I have taken on board what you have told me and see you again soon" speech or blog.

If you have not quite got there, this is the time to really go for it – get your publicity machine working like mad. Approach everyone who is relevant and let them know there are only a few days to go. Review your rewards and more.

And if you are in the lucky position that all is going well and you know you will hit or exceed your target, prepare your "thank you so much" speech or blog and start getting on with delivering what you have promised.

Completion - assuming you have been successful

Depending on the platform you are using, completion will involve different things. With pledges you can expect the money to be transferred, minus the fees, within a couple of weeks. With debt and equity platforms there will also be paperwork to sign and there may be things to register in official places such as Companies House in the UK.

And, let's face it, this is really just the beginning of the project itself, so it might be wise to take the weekend off to recharge your batteries so you are all set to go on Monday morning.

In summary

1.   There are three critical phases to a campaign – planning, preparation and the campaign itself.
2.   Planning is essential and will be the underpinning for your campaign – don't skimp on it.
3.   Crowd funding does not mean you can get away without having a proper plan for your business!
4.   Before choosing your platform, update yourself on what is going on in the crowd, for example via relevant LinkedIn groups.
5.   Gather all the information you will need for your campaign before you start. Keep it near you throughout the campaign in case the crowd has questions for you.
6.   Plan what you are going to do each day during your campaign – have some peak moments of promotional activity and some quieter times so you keep the crowd wanting more.
7.   Remember that the video is the teaser, but it will be the contents of your campaign and the rewards on offer that actually persuade the crowd to back you.
8.   Launch with a big bang – tell *everyone*, issue a press release and tweet like mad for about two days. Then move into phase 2 of your campaign, keeping people updated all the time, but also have blasts of PR activity to keep the crowd interested and encourage new funders to come forward.
9.   You cannot prepare for a completely unexpected crisis, but you should be prepared for most things that could go wrong, especially simple things such as your internet connection breaking!
10. When the campaign is over, and whether it has been successful or not, spend some time reviewing what has happened and take away the lessons you have learned.

Chapter 8

What happens after you have got the money?

Running a successful crowd funding campaign, especially if it is pledge- or equity-based, is a major achievement, as fewer than 50% of campaigns get fully funded. So, if you have been successful, congratulations.

With the money you have raised, you can now get on with delivering the business or project goals you intended. There are now lots of other things to think about.

The first 100 days

All good investors pay a great deal of attention to something they have backed for the first 100 days after they invest. What they tell me is that you never know quite what will happen until after the business has banked the money and had three months to operate. Broadly speaking, businesses perform in one of three ways.

1. They deliver on their promises on time and within cost.
2. They over-deliver on the plan.
3. They fail to deliver on their promises on time and are not in control of costs, with expenditure exceeding what was planned and sales falling behind.

Whatever type of funding you raise, it is worth thinking hard about how you will perform over those 100 days. If you know in your heart that your plan will over-deliver against what you are forecasting, you are probably not being ambitious enough in your fundraising plans. The effect of this is that you will need to raise more money, probably at a time when you are really desperate. If you know that the plan you are offering is unrealistic, stop and rewrite it – it will be even more difficult to raise the money you will need later if your business has failed to deliver and is clearly going more and more wrong every day that passes. If you know you really can deliver what you are promising, then build up as much evidence as you can to prove it, challenge yourself again and again, and get others to double-check your plans. Once you are completely confident, make sure your funders know it.

Spending the money

This might be the first time that you have had so much money available to you at one time. From day one, I recommend that you install real discipline in how you use it. It may even be worth setting up a savings account alongside your day-to-day one and transferring the money into it. You can then withdraw the money you need as you need it, and you will be less tempted to spend it on that "sudden urgent need".

Staying in touch with your funders

With dozens if not hundreds of new supporters, this is your chance to build relationships with all of them. There are some general rules it is worth following from here on in, as you want to keep them as your champions for many years to come.

Stay engaged

Crowd funding is all about building relationships. Keep the good work up and report to them regularly. Or why not set up and run a private LinkedIn group or Facebook page and invite them to join that? Give them the good news quickly and the bad news quicker. Invite them to engage and comment on what you are doing – after all, they are (probably) your first and definitely your most loyal customers and partners. It is a very good idea to have some sort of proactive regular communication with funders such as an e-newsletter. Another good idea is to survey your funders to find out how they think you are doing as the campaign progresses. You can also encourage them to look at your LinkedIn group or Facebook page for updates, and even ask them to follow you on Twitter for immediate news. In some cases, you may wish to invite them to a "funder day" when you meet up with them and tell them all about what you are doing.

Stay passionate and personal, not only telling them what you are up to with the business or project but also your views and opinions on other relevant things, such as industry developments.

Inevitably, you will receive awkward questions from your funders. Some of them may not fully understand what they have backed; others might have a deep knowledge that gives them an advantage over you in what you are doing and may wish to correct you; and some are just plain tricky people. When you get these questions, the trick is always to answer them after you have thought through your reply. Don't be tempted to reply quickly, and never match insult with insult. Think through not only what they are saying but why they are saying it and respond accordingly. If necessary, get an experienced friend or an adviser to look over your reply before you send it — just in case you have said something you shouldn't.

Never forget that some of your severest critics may in fact be your biggest supporters, and also that you never know when you might want to approach them or their friends for more money, favours or contacts in the future.

Ask for their help

Your funders already know a lot about you and what you are up to. Take advantage of this and use it. Ask for their advice and opinions on your products and services via emails, blogs and surveys. Pebble asked its funders for volunteers to test its shipment processes for its product — those lucky individuals received their Pebble watches earlier than everyone else!

Remember your responsibilities

You have an obligation to deliver on the promises you made when you undertook your campaign. Make sure you have a detailed record of what you promised and when you must deliver, and try to make sure you stick to it. If you cannot, give people lots of warning and explain what alternative you would like to offer them.

Legal responsibilities

In the case of debt, equity and social enterprise funding, you also have legal responsibilities.

Alternative asset funding such as invoice auctioning

Typically, you have a responsibility to ensure that the invoice you have raised is paid. Make sure you stay on top of the debt collection – if the payment is delayed you will face fines, and if it is not paid at all you will still be liable to repay the full sum you borrowed from your funders by other means.

Crowd debt

As with all borrowing, you must meet the interest and capital repayments on time. If you do not, and especially if you have provided security for the loan, the platform provider will take steps to recover the money owed, including taking charge if necessary. If you think you are going to face problems because things are not turning out as planned, speak to the platform operator as soon as possible and work together to come up with an alternative plan.

Crowd equity

In legal terms, having external shareholders is a serious responsibility, especially as you will probably be a director of the company. Shareholders have rights and you have obligations, both under the Companies Act and based on what you agreed in the shareholders' agreement. This is on top of any separate contract you may have made with them to provide them with rewards in addition to their investment.

Some of your duties include:

- filing your accounts and annual return at Companies House each year and on time (your accountant will be able to do this for you)
- ensuring that you run the company in its and its shareholders' best interests, not your own
- not overtrading or trading when insolvent
- reporting to your shareholders as agreed.

Social enterprise funding

Remember that if you are fundraising for a charity you will have to meet the rules and regulations of the Charity Commission and the Charities Act on top of everything else. In particular, remember that the Charity Commission is insistent that you should not do anything to damage the reputation of your charity *or* that of any other charity in your sector. You may also face restrictions on the rewards you can offer if your funder or their close connections are benefiting from the charitable purpose of the charity.

If you fundraise for a company limited by guarantee, remember that you cannot distribute the profits by way of dividend or share buy-back to your funders. It is probably a good idea to take some specialist advice as to whether you can legally distribute certain types of reward.

And if things start to go wrong

It is never easy when a business plan starts to go wrong, but there are things you can do to mitigate the problems on the way, and, if the end does come, to manage this well, so that you come out of it with a good reputation rather than a bad one. These are the big things that go wrong and some tips on how to deal with them.

Money

It is said in the venture capital world that venture-backed companies always need more money. They either need it because things are going much better than expected and therefore everyone wants to push forward more quickly, or, more likely, because things are going worse than expected. There are four simple tricks to making sure you do not run out of money.

1. Always have a contingency amount in your fundraising to cover unexpected emergencies. Typically this should be 10% on top of the funding you need to deliver the plan.
2. Keep absolute control over spending and, as the founder, you should know at the end of every day how much cash you have in the bank, how much you are waiting to be paid by customers and how much you owe. Make sure you have a system that can give you this information every evening.
3. Have a rough-and-ready new fundraising pitch tucked away somewhere that you can pull out and update very quickly if you need to. Remember to update it regularly so that it is in pretty good shape if you ever need it.
4. Keep tabs on who will back you the next time around – this might be your current backers, new crowd funders, angels, venture capitalists or even, dare I say it, a bank. Make sure that these people are always kept particularly up to date on how you are doing and what you are planning, so that when you need them they are there for you.

The team collapses

The crowd world is young, so there is little evidence of what the long-term impact this type of fundraising will have on the teams that build businesses. However, you can be sure that raising money will have the effect of changing the team. It may grow, it may even shrink, but it is almost certain it will go through extremely stressful times, and with stress comes the risk of the team breaking up.

As the founder, you need to be ready for this and always ready for damage limitation. In particular, try to make sure that your own ambitions don't mean that you are the one who causes it all to fall over. Do remember, though, that while teams do collapse, there are lots of other people out there who can also do the jobs of those who have departed. And also remember that you may have decided today that you really loathe someone and would rather they were banished to a desert island, but life is long and one day you may feel differently and want to be friends with them again.

So, however much you dislike someone, do your best to make sure the departure is professionally managed and that they are treated with courtesy at all times. If you are the one staying, be as civilised as possible. Find a friend who is outside the business (and whom you trust) to yell and scream at rather than the person who is going. And absolutely make sure that any departure is properly tied up from a legal point of view. The last thing you need tomorrow, for example, will be a disgruntled ex-co-founder who is still a shareholder and will use their shareholding to be as obstructive as possible.

The product does not work – the vital importance of pivoting

Most great entrepreneurs have failed many times. They become great because the total of all their eventual successes outweighs their failures in the memories of the public. They also carry on and keep adapting until they get things right, even if this means dumping the current project and doing something new. Take comfort from that. Funders understand this and it is part of the risk they take. (It is also one of the reasons why venture investing is so exciting!) If you are honest and open with your funders, there is no reason why they will blame you for an honest failure – you may even find that they are more willing to back you next time around because they see that you have learned from your experiences.

So don't get blinkered about what you are doing. As they say, if it looks like a fish and smells like a fish, it's a fish. If your product is not working and cannot work, it won't work just because you won't give up. To avoid getting to the end of the line, keep re-evaluating what you are doing and adjusting all the time to make sure your product is going to be something that people will want ... and will buy at a price that generates profits for you.

Even if things do not work out, it may be possible to "pivot" your business into a new area. Take a look around the sector you are operating in and see what you can salvage and use for a new, related project. If you have created something that does not sell to your expected customers, it may also be worth seeing whether there are other people who would like it – possibly at a different price point.

Crises

Sometimes events occur that you cannot do anything about. There could be a fire in your warehouse that destroys all your stock, your main supplier could go out of business, your co-founder could be hospitalised because of a serious accident, or there could be a big economic shock like the credit crunch that paralyses everything. There are some simple things you can do to mitigate unforeseen crises. One thing is to take out insurance against certain eventualities. Another way to cushion yourself is to keep a war chest of money tucked away so that you can tide your business over until you find a new way forward. But the best way to avoid being ruined by a crisis is to have a good group of people around you who can help you through. So always respect and stay close to your inside crowd, so that when you need them they are there for you.

In summary

1. The real work starts after your campaign has completed.
2. The first 100 days after your campaign will be the time when you and your funders find out whether you will exceed your plans, keep on track or find things are not going as well as expected.
3. Keep a close eye on the money you have and don't get carried away. Spend cautiously and in line with your plan.
4. Stay engaged with your funders, telling them how things are going and managing their expectations, for example about when their reward will be delivered. Feel free to ask for their help with things such as more market research.
5. Remember you have legal responsibilities; for example, if you borrow you are obliged to pay the interest and capital in line with the agreement you signed. If you fail to meet your responsibilities, people may take legal action against you.

6. Keep your contingency money safe for emergencies.
7. If your team does not work out, don't worry – but find more people to help you as soon as possible.
8. If the product does not work, learn from what has happened and be honest with your funders about what has happened.
9. Why not try to take what you have learned and "pivot" into a new area, if you can.
10. There are some crises you cannot recover from, but if you keep a good team around you, keep your crowd supportive and keep some money back for a rainy day, then the world should not end for you.

Part Three

Investing money in the crowd

Chapter 9

Who is in the crowd?

The crowd is an amazing collection of people who have been inspired to help you achieve your goals. The people who invest range from complete novices who have never invested before and want to play with a bit of spare cash that they have (this type of people are most often found on pledge platforms) to super-sophisticated and experienced investors (typically found on equity and debt platforms). It's worth noting upfront that on many debt and equity sites, the broad regulatory framework in most western economies means that these individuals have signed certificates declaring that they know what they are doing when it comes to investing – these are often known as sophisticated or high net worth investor certificates.

When I started writing this book, it seemed a good idea to look a bit deeper into who invests, and so in autumn 2012 I undertook a big survey of a couple of hundred crowd investors and asked them to tell us all about themselves. I put the survey out into the crowd via various LinkedIn groups, Facebook and Twitter, and I also emailed all the angels I know with a link, asking them to complete it. The reward for completing the survey was a free copy of this book!

I looked at what they told me and it has become clear that there are many types of investor. I have described them as follows, based on what they told me and how I see it.

The different types of crowd investor

The gambler

Some crowd investors enjoy the gamble they are taking with your business. They do not invest more than they can afford to lose but they bet on what they see to be the best chances. They will be highly affected by form, judging the quality of different campaigns and investing in the best opportunity they can find.

The hobby investor

Hobby investors dabble in crowd funding. They spend the spare cash they have, when they have it. Typically they invest small sums – probably around £50 but perhaps up to a couple of hundred pounds. Crowd investing provides them with an interesting occupation in their spare time; they like to feel they are doing some good and they appreciate the rewards they receive.

The crowd evangelist

As true converts to crowd funding, evangelists take their investing very seriously. They invest all the time, typically small sums, in a large variety of projects.

The philanthropist

Some investors really invest to give something back. They do not have high expectations of rewards and are not particularly motivated by returns.

The business angel

Business angels make great crowd investors because they really do think like an investor. They will focus on all the important issues that make a business succeed: the team, the plan, the business model and so on. Typically they will invest largish sums of money – one recently put £100,000 into a crowd campaign, but most would typically invest £5,000 to £10,000. Expect them to ask serious questions and to take their time to hand over the money. They will stay involved after you close your campaign and can be incredibly helpful to you, providing advice and contacts that will help you grow the business. Some may even offer to roll up their sleeves and help you with day-to-day challenges and opportunities.

The private investor

Private investors take their investing seriously and invest with the intention of getting their money back and making more money on top. They are different from angels in that they are typically passive investors and do not get involved with the company on a day-to-day basis. Even if they are quiet, do not assume private investors are stupid. They are often very savvy crowd funders who know exactly what they are doing.

The crowd entrepreneur

Many entrepreneurs hang out in the crowd and will back (usually with small sums) other businesses or projects in the same or even in a different space. On Kickstarter this has been formalised into the Kickstarter Forward model, where all successful crowd-funded businesses and projects agree to reinvest 5% of their net profits, once their own company is profitable, into other Kickstarter projects.

The institutional investor

Increasingly, professional investors who look after other people's money are arriving in the crowd. The most prevalent example is Family Offices (private companies who manage the finances of a single wealthy family) who are adopting areas such as invoice auctioning as one of the asset classes they invest in.

The international investor

It's not just Americans who are taking crowd investing into their hearts. Investors from the Middle East and elsewhere – always on the hunt for opportunities in western economies – are now appearing in the crowd. Like institutional investors, they invest for a reason – to get a superior return from a more reliable asset.

FAQs about crowd investors

Why do they invest?

In the survey I conducted of investors in crowd funding platforms, most investors (approximately 64%) told me they have got involved in crowd funding because they see it as an innovative model through which they can help finance projects or SMEs. Around 44% do so because they are curious about it, whereas, interestingly, only 20% are on the hunt for better returns. This suggests that the social motive is currently the primary reason for investing via the crowd, although a few people seem to think it is a good way to break free of established financing channels such as the banks.

What do they invest in?

Over 70% of investors in the crowd invest or want to invest in early stage businesses, with 61% interested in start-ups and 39% in established businesses. Around 40% like the idea of creative projects, but far smaller numbers are particularly interested in other specific sectors. However, only around 10% are interested in investing across all sectors. This suggests that crowd funding, as it matures, will prove suitable for fundraising projects and businesses across all sectors, with investors who want to focus on specific sectors looking across different platforms for deals. Our research also suggested that we will see more and more activity in the equity and debt sectors, though whether this ends up being at the expense of the pledge-based sector or in addition to it we do not yet know.

In order of priority, investors hand over money because they like:

- how the money will be used (68%)
- the sector (65%)
- the terms and likely returns (55%)
- the pitch (55%)
- the summary (35%)
- the online engagement (23%)
- the fact that it is local (20%)
- the rewards (20%)
- the video (18%).

Investors also told me that the team is very important.

What this tells me is that if a fundraising does not have a decent underpinning of what is generally called "the investment case", no amount of fancy marketing will help get the fundraising started. That being said, having the right extras will make a difference, and your presentation of the investment case is important. When you look at lots of difference pitches on various platforms, you immediately see that those which look amateurish instil less confidence than those that look polished. Whatever they may say, the evidence suggests that investors are still very influenced by a well presented pitch.

How much do they invest and how often?

Our survey was very revealing on this. Firstly, it is clear that investors invest different amounts depending on the type of investment they are making, with pledge fundraising typically receiving around £30–£50 per investor but equity ones receiving £1,000–£10,000.

Overall, investors seem to be allocating around £1,000–£2,000 a year, with a small number putting up between £20,000 and £50,000 and a tiny number becoming pretty serious at £100,000.

Some people invest regularly, usually monthly, but there is still a large number who invest on a more *ad hoc* basis. The underlying message seems to be that most investors do not invest randomly or on a whim but, even with quite small sums, take their investing seriously.

What do they want out of it?

Generally, on pledge-based platforms, investors want to get the rewards they are promised when they make their pledge.

When it comes to debt, investors want a return that is over and above what a more traditional bank would give them and one that reflects the risk they are taking on lending the money – i.e. the bank base rate plus a percentage. At the moment, the total return they appear to want is around 10% per year, but some investors seem to be happy with around 5%–7% and a few want well over this.

When it comes to crowd equity, most investors told me that on the sale of the business they want a rate of return that is equivalent to 25% per year for every year they have been investing, although some would be happy with 10%–15%. Some expressed this in terms of the "multiple of money" they want back; these people ranged from wanting twice to 10 times their money.

Where are they investing?

This is always a challenging question to answer. The truth is that they are investing all over the place, but the websites they particularly mention are:

- Kickstarter and IndieGoGo – pledge
- Crowdcube and Seedrs – equity
- ThinCats, Funding Circle, Kiva and Zopa – debt.

Another sign of where investors hang out can be uncovered by a quick look at the various crowd platforms. Crowdcube claims to have over 37,000 registered users.

Do investors really understand crowd investing?

From the responses to our survey, I would say a wholehearted yes. The great test for understanding is whether people know what it really costs to make one sort of investment over another. The survey revealed that investors know about and accept the typical 5% fee on funds raised charged by platform operators.

How do people become crowd investors?

Most investors have become involved in crowd funding in only the last couple of years. The upsurge in interest has grown and grown since then, with more and more people joining all the time, either being recommended to do it by friends or because they are seeing the success of it in funding projects and businesses via word of mouth or PR. Online news and searches are the places where most people first hear about crowd funding. What tickles their interest is the wide variety of opportunities on offer and the ease with which you can invest.

There are still a lot of investors who have registered with sites but have not yet invested – my survey suggested that just over 25% are still deciding whether or not to hand over any money to fundraisers. And, for most of them, the crowd is still a tiny part of their overall investing activities.

What is the crowd concerned about?

All the usual things that all investors worry about! The big issue is whether the crowd will deliver the returns that investors would like to see. I have particularly noticed that investors are concerned that the valuation of shares being sold on crowd equity platforms may be too high, and that the returns on the debt platforms may not be as good as they first appear. There are also fears that crowd funding really isn't suitable for some types of company, especially very high-tech ones.

The surveyed investors told me that they have some specific concerns. Will equity fundraisers be able to manage their large shareholder lists? Will the lack of a regulatory structure that fits with the characteristics of the crowd be a serious problem? Many, but by no means all, feel that debt fundraisings are still the safer way for an investor to back an SME, rather than using an equity platform.

However, for every champion of one type of platform there are others who feel differently. As one investor said when I asked which type of crowd funding was best for them:

> "Donations. Equity is pointless as there is generally no exit in sight and being part of a huge number of shareholders is problematic."

To be honest, in both debt and equity the markets are so young that it is impossible to tell yet whether these fears will be justified. And how the pledge-based models will evolve as other platforms mature is also anyone's guess.

What types of crowd funding are the most attractive to investors?

I started to write this book because of my experience in angel investing; the arrival of Crowdcube and Seedrs in the UK market made it very clear that something new was now on offer to angels. So it was very interesting when investors told me that providing debt funding is, today, marginally more attractive than equity funding. Some 48% of investors are engaged in debt lending and 19% in alternative debt lending, such as invoice or asset finance platforms. This compares with 46% of investors engaged in ordinary equity platforms and 21% in platforms that offer alternative equity propositions such as convertible or preference shares. However, both types of investing have overtaken pledge-based routes: 44% of investors are engaged in donations and 17% in enhanced donation platforms.

Is the crowd an intrinsically dangerous place for investors?

"Yes!" yell the sceptics. "No!" shout the evangelists. The truth, of course, is that it all depends. Certainly, from what I have found from looking at the market and talking to entrepreneurs, investors and those who have the most to win or lose – the people running businesses that operate crowdfunding platforms – everyone takes the issues that might make the crowd dangerous very seriously. Generally, people increasingly want proper rules and regulations to be put in place to ensure the orderly running of the market. Indeed, the UK Crowdfunding Association is trying to encourage the government to create a new regulatory framework for crowd funding, and it appears that the government and the FCA are now responsive to this wish. Investors largely want the market to do the obvious things that protect them – they particularly like the idea of having an escrow account (i.e. a separate bank account where the money sits) for the money being raised, which cannot be touched by the entrepreneur until the fundraising is completed. And one of the most interesting comments in the survey came from an investor who suggested that peer review would be the most effective way to ensure that people behave themselves.

A good number of investors also tell me that at the end of the day it is up to the investor to understand the risks of this type of investing and that they should act accordingly. Some felt that as long as the sums invested are very small, then the dangers are, by default, limited. The overall message continues to be "don't invest more than you can afford to lose".

This investor summed it up:

> "The government's track record on the regulation of lending institutions is not great in recent years and I fear that if they get their fingers into the crowd funding market then they will mess it up. As long as investors are cautious and spread their risk they are reasonably well protected. The same rules as other 'angel'-type investments apply: if you don't understand the proposition – Don't Invest; if you are not sure – Don't Invest; if you feel the need to ask a question – Ask It; spread your risk and if in any doubt – Don't Invest."

Will investors make returns from the crowd?

This is the big question, really. If investors cannot get something back from investing via the crowd, the market will die. When it comes to pledge platforms, the investor mood music seems pretty positive, with a general view that most fundraisings do deliver the products or services pledged, even if this takes longer than might have been expected. As far as debt is concerned, the track record of borrowers is fairly good. Typically, interest and capital payments get made, and when problems do arise, the platform operators deal with them and look to deliver on the promises they made to lenders, for example by recovering security to pay off the loan. When it comes to equity, the jury is still out – I am not aware at the date of writing that any of the companies that have completed equity fundraising have yet exited. So we wait and see.

In summary

1. There are lots of different types of crowd investor – depending on what funding you are looking for, you will come across different types.

2. Different investors want different things – you can influence which investors you get by what you offer them.
3. Most investors will want some sort of reward, even if it is only feeling really good about what they are doing. Make sure you can stick to your promises and deliver.
4. Investors invest on debt and equity crowd platforms to get better returns than they could get by investing in other asset classes or by putting their money in the bank. For you, this means that the money you raise could be expensive.
5. Investors invest wildly different amounts for all sorts of reasons – do not try to second-guess how much people will invest, but focus on giving them something they really want for the money they will give you.
6. If you are using crowd equity, remember you are selling shares for money and you will be in a relationship with your investors, probably for many, many years.
7. Ensure that your backers understand how their money will be used and give them reassurance that it will be spent on what they think it will be spent on. Then make sure you do what you promise.
8. Remember that investors look through the glitz to the underlying story. Your video is only the teaser – they will actually back you based on the strength of the case you make for why you need their money.
9. Many investors have concerns about the risks involved with crowd funding, especially around crowd equity platforms because this is a relatively new form of investing. There are many people who are very concerned about fraud on pledge and donation platforms. Make sure you understand and obey the legal rules so that investors are comfortable that you will not rip them off.
10. Look after your investors and they will look after you. Remember that you never know when you might need them and that your internet footprint means that they will be able to find you!

Chapter 10

How to invest as part of the crowd

Whatever type of investor you are, it's a good idea to follow a process when it comes to investing, so that you don't kick yourself afterwards if it does not work out as planned.

These are the rules for investing in crowd equity set by Kayar Raghavan, who backed Seedrs. Many of them are just as applicable for investing in other types of crowd funding, though perhaps in other areas there's less need to get really close to the entrepreneur.

Kayar Raghavan's rules for crowd equity investing

1. Invest in a start-up only if you fully understand the subject/concept/idea of the business.
2. Invest only if you can get to know the entrepreneur well and are comfortable with his style, reasonableness, coachability, emotional intelligence and ability to accept and manage peaks and troughs and the rough and tumble of start-up businesses.
3. Invest no more than what you can risk.
4. Invest only if you can see a way to exit in four to five years (even if you don't intend exiting).
5. It will help to know fellow investors in advance and ensure that all their objectives, at least at a high level, are in sync.

6. Numbers and valuation may be important, but place a premium on the term sheet (the document used by investors to make their offer, which includes everything from the valuation they are placing on the company to specific requirements such as how many directors the company is to have and how they will be appointed), the cap table (the document that lists all the investors, the shares and loans they have and how much they have invested and/or lent) and the contract and read them carefully to ensure full understanding and comfort and to avoid nasty surprises later.

How much to invest

The first step to investing is to decide how much you would like to invest overall and over what time period. Pretty much anything goes in the crowd, so there are no particular rules as to how much you should or shouldn't invest, but for your own peace of mind it probably pays to decide ranges of money you will invest in different types of campaign. I cannot repeat too often that the overall rule you must apply is never to invest more than you can afford to lose.

The amounts invested by the crowd investors I surveyed range widely, from £50–£100 a month to £50,000 a year. Usually, but not always, crowd equity investments are larger than pledges or reward-based funding because the nature of that type of funding makes it more economical to invest in larger amounts. Also, some tax break schemes such as EIS have a minimum investment threshold.

On some platforms, especially the debt crowd ones, you can send the platform a fixed sum and ask them to spread it equally across all the fundraising campaigns they carry. Kevin Caley, the founder of ThinCats, has told me that he is seeing investors place tens of thousands of pounds at a time on his platform.

One thing to think about when you do contribute to a campaign, especially an equity one, is how much of the cake you want for yourself.

In the angel world, larger equity stakes in a business tend to carry with them more influence and extra rights. These might include:

- a seat on the board
- the opportunity to buy additional shares today or in the future at a discounted price
- the right to approve or disapprove such things as management employment packages, the appointment of management and major items of capital expenditure.

Whatever you decide, remember that this is very high-risk investing and that you should *never* invest more than a total of 10% of your free assets (i.e. your assets outside your home and pension capital) in the crowd funding asset class.

Will your money be used?

Around 40%–50% of campaigns on any one platform will be unsuccessful, so you will need to work into your calculations that some of the campaigns you support will fail and therefore your money will be returned to you. Of course, even if the campaign is not successful, you can approach the company direct; however, in all likelihood if the crowd has not funded it there is probably something pretty fundamental that the campaigner still needs to do to optimise the business or project, and therefore you should be wary of pursuing this route. Instead, you will be able to invest this money in another campaign that will hopefully be even better than the last one.

What types of crowd funding will suit you?

The great variety of types of funding now being sought in the crowd means that as an investor the choice is yours – well, almost. Some sites, particularly the alternative debt funding sites, are not very interested in very small investors. Other sites have restrictions based on things such as your nationality; for example, US citizens are not generally allowed to invest in campaigns based outside the US. It is worth checking with the platform provider if they have any terms and conditions that you as the investor will have to meet before you start investing.

The next step is to decide what types of return you want. If you are most interested in funding companies by effectively pre-ordering their products or services, then pledge platforms such as Crowdfunder, Kickstarter or IndieGoGo are the ones for you. If you are looking to get regular income you should head towards the debt platforms such as Funding Circle, Funding Knight and ThinCats. And if you are prepared to wait for a potentially bumper return, head to the crowd equity sites such as Crowdcube and Seedrs.

Many people in the crowd told me that they spread their money across many types of funding, so don't feel you have to stick to just one type.

Which businesses or projects should you choose?

Whether you choose one platform or many, the next step is to create some rules for yourself and what you will and won't fund.

Some crowd funders told me that they like to invest locally, others that they like to back certain sectors, and still others that they only choose those initiatives that have the best chance of success.

The great news about crowd funding is that at last you can build a portfolio of investments in a very affordable way. So there is a real opportunity for the "ordinary" investor to build a portfolio just like the venture capitalists. With a diversified portfolio you will get failures, but you are also more likely to get a big success. You might be interested to know that all the research suggests that you need a portfolio of around 30 investments to get the best chance of finding three really big winners, so if you are going to be a crowd investor think big in terms of the number of investments you are going to make.

What to look out for

There are lots of things to look into when you are crowd investing, and it should be fun, enjoyable and interesting doing your research, especially in today's internet-enabled world. To be honest, if you find it boring and a waste of your time investigating what you are going to spend your money on, crowd funding probably isn't for you.

The overall rule of any type of investment or pledge is that the buyer should beware. The vast majority of fundraisers on crowd platforms are honest, decent people and businesses looking to get money to achieve their goals, but you always need to bear in mind that there are fraudsters out there too, and there are also honest people who will fail despite their best intentions – this is why you must do some research before you invest.

Here are the things to look for. A well presented pitch will be very attractive and the fact that the fundraiser has gone to the effort to make their pitch look good should be a point in their favour, but it is what's behind the groovy video and smooth words that you should pay most attention to.

The investment case

The single most important thing to look out for after a pitch has caught your attention is the investment case, i.e. the explanation by the fundraiser of what money they need, why they need it, how they are going to use it, what results this will get and what they will give you in return for you handing over your money. Thanks to the way in which crowd platforms supply you with information, you may have to dig out the full investment case by reading all the documents and watching the video to get a full picture. As you investigate the investment case, think about whether it all adds up.

Key questions to ask include the following.

- Is the story consistent?
- Will there be enough money to do the job?
- Does the team appear capable of delivering?

- Is there any proof that there is going to be a demand for the product or service being developed?
- Can the stuff needed to make it happen all be brought together in such a way that everything does get delivered?

The team

It is said in the venture capital world that an A team can always find a way to deliver a B-class product, but that there is no certainty that a B team will be able to deliver an A-class product. And very few angels or venture capitalists would disagree with this statement. The questions are, of course, what makes an A team and will an A team stay on top form in the short, medium and long term. Equally, investors always have to ask themselves whether a B team can develop into an A team with the right tweaks and/or training.

I cannot tell you how many investors I have known over the years who have handed over sums of money, at levels at which they would not give to their closest friends or family, to relative strangers without doing proper checks on them – and have lived to regret it.

Don't be tempted to ignore this. Always spend a lot of time looking hard at the people who are raising the money. Check them out on LinkedIn, Twitter, etc., take up references, but, most of all, connect with them yourself. Tweet them, email them, speak to them and do it a lot so you get a real feel for what they are like and whether they are the sort of people you want to have your money. The more time you spend with them, the greater sense you will get about whether they are:

- consistent (good) or changeable (bad)
- savvy (good) or naïve (bad)
- reliable (good) or flaky (bad)
- their own person (good) or too dependent on others (bad)
- a team player (good) or a prima donna (usually but not always bad, depending on their level of genius!).

All of this matters, because the only certainty is that if they are the wrong people for you, you are unlikely to get back from them what you want.

Teams work best with a balance of people with different personalities and experiences, but each team should have at least:

- the innovator, inventor or entrepreneur – who should not necessarily be the chief executive officer (CEO)
- a CEO or managing director who will co-ordinate everything and keep the whole show on the road
- a salesman who may or may not also be good at marketing
- if the salesman is not good at marketing, a marketing expert
- someone who looks after the money – not necessarily a finance director early on, but certainly a financial controller who is responsible for the books
- advisers – they may be formally appointed or just in the background, but all good entrepreneurial teams know they need to take advice to get ahead, and not just from people such as accountants and lawyers but also from business people who have done it before.

One last thing to remember about people is that if the platform is charging the entrepreneur and not you, then legally the entrepreneur is the platform's client, not you, and you should therefore not assume that the platform is automatically acting in your best interests.

The business model

Most industries have certain business models that usually succeed and others that rarely do. When you are thinking about an opportunity, do some digging to see if the model the fundraisers are planning to use has a track record of success in that sector. Challenge this aspect of the pitch with the fundraiser to get a better understanding of why they are pursuing the model they have chosen.

It's also worth looking at things such as typical sales and production cycles in the sector and also – something that many people don't think about – the supply chain and how robust it is; investors and even entrepreneurs can get a bit dreamy when it comes to looking at whether the product or service can actually be delivered to specification day in day out, 365 days a year. And if it cannot be, then the immediate impact will be on cash, since the business will start gobbling it up to deal with the problems that arise.

The intellectual property

IP is all the stuff that a business has that makes it unique. Some businesses are rich in formal IP such as patents, trademarks and design rights. Think about Apple and you will immediately know what I mean. But all companies have something that makes them different and you need to know what that something is and whether it can be copied or crushed easily by competitors, because in business if there is a golden egg, you can be sure that a giant will try to take it from you if they can. And you need to be aware that in some cases other companies or people own IP that can stop someone else from doing something.

So look hard at the IP that a fundraiser is claiming to have and make sure it all adds up. And bear in mind that even if you are doing a pledge fundraising for a product, there's the risk that if the company does not own the IP rights of the product they are promising to deliver, you could find that someone who does have that IP will wade in and stop them delivering it to you.

The financials

There are four main rules when it comes to looking at the financials of a project or business.

1. The only thing you can be certain of is that the real numbers that play out will be either better or worse than the financial projections you are shown when you invest.
2. With Excel spreadsheet software there is no excuse for the financial projections not to look absolutely perfect.
3. Most projects fail because they do not have enough money to deliver and keep delivering.
4. It is very hard to get profit margins to rise as customers always want to pay less and suppliers always want to charge more.

So when it comes to digging around in the financial projections, use your common sense. Clearly, more experienced entrepreneurs will be better at preparing numbers and those who have advisers helping them definitely will. What you need to look at is what is behind the numbers you are being shown – the assumptions made and who prepared them.

Market demand and timing

When it comes to market demand there are three main things to think about.

1. Is this a sector that is growing steadily, or is it likely to grow or collapse explosively at some point?
2. When are changes likely to take place in the market and where is the opportunity positioned in this timeline?
3. How much does the product or service solve a problem that has not yet been solved (and how big is that problem)? Or is it just making life easier or quicker for the customer?

Timing in business is everything. When it comes to entrepreneurial businesses, some fill a long-term need and make steady profits and growth – the best of them generate cash profits of 10%–20% year in, year out. And some businesses have amazing success by spotting a short-term opportunity, exploiting it and then moving on – the most obvious example of this is retailers who gear up for Christmas each year, but by Boxing Day have the decorations down and are into sale mode.

When you are looking to back a crowd fundraising, think hard about timing, as no amount of money will solve the fact that the market opportunity has been missed.

Sales and marketing

The best entrepreneurs are typically brilliant at sales and marketing and often out-compete more old-fashioned business people and practices. If an entrepreneur has chosen crowd funding as a route to get money to grow, it is a very good sign that they have "got" the message that they need to be out there selling and promoting what they are doing. How an entrepreneur conducts that campaign will tell you a lot about how good they are at sales and marketing. If they are on the ball, actively marketing their campaign all the time, being responsive to questions and queries and everything else a campaign entails, you can take comfort from the fact that they will probably also deliver when the campaign has closed. If their pitch is a one-hit wonder and is followed by virtual silence, then you should start to worry.

Smaller things

There are a few smaller things to think about when considering a campaign.

- My pet bug bear is sloppy use of language and spelling mistakes – especially in headings! To my mind, this is a sign of a poorly thought-through proposal and would discourage me from investing.
- If a team is completely new to what they are doing, I like to see evidence of where they have shown signs of both entrepreneurialism and hard graft in other areas of their life.
- Watch out for minor inconsistencies between things such as the business plan and what is being said in the video.

Anonymity

The first instinct of most people is to reveal who they are, but when it comes to crowd funding, it is more than possible to be an investor without revealing your identity to the crowd. Certain types of crowd funding, such as crowd debt, will by default keep your identity anonymous, although the operator will, of course, have to know who you are and will make checks to ensure that you are who you say you are for legal reasons, such as the prevention of money laundering.

When it comes to donation or pledge funding, even though the platform operator will know who you are, as will the people receiving your pledges, it is perfectly possible to have a pseudonym in the crowd that you use as your identity when you make a pledge or a comment. If you are going to go down this route, remember that you can be caught out. Also, if you stick out from the crowd too much, quite a lot of people will be very keen to find out who you really are and will take steps to satisfy their curiosity.

Crowd equity is where you have to be most aware about your identity. Remember that if you become a shareholder in a company, this information is recorded (in the UK) at Companies House. Make sure that if you want to remain as private as possible you do not inadvertently buy some shares in a company and then find that your home address becomes a matter of public record. I suggest that if you are wealthy, it would be wise to seek professional advice from your wealth manager and other advisers as to the approach you should take in the crowd.

Becoming a champion for a crowd funding campaign

One of the points of getting involved in crowd funding is that you participate and engage with the projects or businesses that you back. I would thoroughly recommend that, if you do back something, you stay very engaged with it.

Being engaged, though, can take very different forms. Some people prefer to pledge or invest and then keep a watching eye from the side lines; others will actively engage with the fundraisers directly but privately; another group will actively engage in public, for example by posting questions and comments on message boards; and the final group will become proactive champions for the people they back.

Interestingly, as crowd funding develops, we are beginning to see some themes emerging about how public investors want to become. In the alternative debt crowd world, they tend to be very secretive indeed, with few if any even willing to be quoted about their investing activity. In stark contrast, it is positively cool to be public and vocal on the donation and pledge sites. In the social enterprise space there is a tendency for funders to take a positive pride in being associated with using their money to "do good".

As an investor, you are free to do what you like. You might wish to be well known as an investor on Kickstarter, but keep completely silent about the fact that you invest on ThinCats. The main point to remember is that if you are noisy but disguised on one platform, but noisy and well known on another, there may come a time when other people join the dots and expose you. I suggest you maintain a consistent persona in the crowd. If you stand out, by making sudden big investments at random intervals, for example, you will provoke the crowd's curiosity!

If you want to become a big investor, it would be well worth your while to get in touch with the platform operators and let them know your intentions, as they may be able to give you extra help with your investing.

If you decide to become a very vocal champion for a campaign, you need to remember that there will be risks, especially if things go wrong in the future. You need to think carefully before you encourage friends, acquaintances and the friends of friends to hand over money for something. Remember that in these days of Twitter *et al.*, it is dangerously easy to influence a fundraising campaign without really meaning to. So as part of your investing strategy, have a think early on about this issue and decide what approach you would like to take in the short, medium and long term.

I also recommend that you prepare yourself for questions that both campaigners and the crowd might have for you. It might be worth jotting down some of the obvious questions you might get asked by an inquisitive individual or even a journalist and preparing some standard answers to them, so that if the need arises you are prepared.

Some of the questions you might well be asked are as follows.

- Who are you and what have you done before now?
- How did you make your money?
- How much money do you have/have available to invest?
- Why are you a crowd investor?
- What investing success stories can you tell me about?
- What investing horror stories can you tell me about?

Remember that it is OK to answer any of these questions with a non-committal reply such as: "That is information I keep private." However, you should never give a rude answer.

In summary

1. Set yourself a strategy for how you are going to invest before you start. If that strategy does not work you can change it, but having no strategy at all is foolish.
2. Invest in what you understand. Not all types of crowd funding will be for you.
3. Never invest more than you can afford to lose.
4. Before you hand over any money, make sure you understand what return you are going to get – even if it is only the feel-good factor.
5. Listen to the crowd and be wary of backing unreferenced strangers.
6. Don't get blinded by the glitz – read the campaign properly, do background checks on the people and the offer, compare and contrast one campaign with another, pay attention to the campaign as it proceeds and make sure you stay in touch after it has completed.
7. Remember that the team is the most important issue. An A team can make a B-grade project successful, but a B team might well destroy an A-grade project.
8. Trust your instinct. If something doesn't feel right, don't invest.
9. If you are not enjoying what you are doing, *stop.*
10. Remember that while it is good to encourage your friends to get involved, you will have to deal with the flak from them if something you got them into goes wrong at a later date.

Chapter 11

What happens after you have invested?

Your role as a funder will be very different depending on what type of investment you have made.

Donation platforms

If you have made a donation you will not receive any reward. However, you can expect the fundraiser to remain in touch with you to keep you updated on how their project is developing.

Donors' views

One respondent to our survey thought that all crowd funding should be donation-based, as they did not like the idea of crowd businesses being obliged to hit targets to make the donors happy.

Another respondent said:

> "Donation-based/reward-based crowd funding works well – it's internationally scalable, legal and encourages philanthropy and good-feeling."

Pledge platforms

If you have made a pledge, you have two choices: to remain passive and just wait for your reward to turn up, or to actively engage with the fundraiser as the project evolves. The best fundraisers will thank you for your pledge, proactively tell you what is going on and invite your comments and contributions all the way through. On platforms such as Kickstarter, up to 70% of funders tend to be entirely passive, but the remaining 30% engage actively on the message boards and so on. In the case of the Pebble watch, the fundraising team has made good use of its funders, asking them questions and for help. It is well worth engaging with the fundraisers while they are getting the project completed as you can make useful contributions that may even make the final product better than originally envisaged.

Actually getting the reward you have been promised is very satisfying, especially if it is for a creative or technology project. If it is music or the arts, you may find yourself being invited to previews or, if your pledge was generous enough, having a private lunch or dinner with the funders or even with a celebrity, such as one of the stars of the show.

Pledge funders' views

Do you remember the quote from one investor in the last chapter who liked donation fundings but not other ones. This is his expanded comment:

> "Donations. Equity is pointless as there is generally no exit in sight and being part of a huge number of shareholders is problematic. Loans are too limited in size; the businesses are unattractive as they need to have been trading for two years yet are raising small amounts of growth capital and the risks look high. In all cases the platform takes no risk of liability yet always gets paid first, like an investment manager!"

Another one said:

> *"I like enhanced donations — if that's where you class Kickstarter and similar platforms that concentrate on pre-sales. The most important aspect is that the project probes the support of interested parties to actually purchase the item being proposed. This is the best type of market research."*

However, not everyone feels the same. As one person told me:

> *"Lending is great. Kickstarter isn't that good as I don't think people understand the risks and just assume that the benefactor will deliver what they say when quite often they may not."*

And someone else said:

> *"Donations leave no control of business."*

Debt and alternative debt platforms

With debt funding, you can expect to receive the payments of interest and capital in line with the agreement you have made. Payments will typically be made into your bank account or into the trading account you have set up on the platform. If it is the latter, you can withdraw the money back into your bank account any time you like. You can also expect to receive statements and reports from the platform operator on how the loan is performing.

You need to be conscious that you will have to pay tax on the income you receive on the loans you have made. You have to declare this on your annual tax return; I understand that in the UK, HMRC is in discussions with platform operators about how it can record who is earning interest on the loans. So while interest payments are currently paid gross (i.e. before any tax is paid) to lenders, there may come a time when the tax authorities obtain the right to deduct tax at source (i.e. before you receive your payment).

If the loan stops performing, usually the platform operator will engage in negotiations with the borrower to try to ensure that the interest and capital repayments will recommence, but ultimately you, as the lender, have a legal right to call in your loan from the borrower and require repayment of the capital and any interest you should be paid.

According to Funding Circle, around 3%–4% of loans will become bad debts, but this figure varies widely depending on the riskiness of the loan made – the estimated lifetime bad debt of the least risky loans is 1.1%, but for those made to more risky businesses it is 4.2%.

Depending on whether the loan is secured, you may or may not get your money back. In the case of Funding Circle, there have been around £1.1m of bad debts, where the borrower has not been able to recover their money, out of the £71.8m of lending made so far. More importantly, only £72,000 of recoveries has been made on loans that have failed, as the loans are unsecured. However, ThinCats told me that because its loans are secured, there is a good chance that lenders will get their money back on bad debts even if this takes some time to achieve. The platform operator will go through a full debt recovery process to release the security that has been offered against the loan and then realise cash from the sale of that security so that the original loan monies (and possibly the outstanding interest owed) can be returned to the investors.

Investors' views

Mark Barry-Jackson and Daniela Sheppard, two investors from Funding Circle who have profiles on the platform's website, both state that they like the concept of helping small businesses by lending to them and are very happy with their average gross yields of 9.5% and 7.8% respectively.

Equity platforms

If you become an equity funder, life is much more interesting and exciting. By investing you become the legal owner of a stake in the business. Ultimately you are now waiting for the cash rewards to start flowing in. It is highly unlikely that you will see any cash for at least three years – in the angel world it is not uncommon for your final exit to take 10 years to achieve.

Remember that if you invest using a tax break scheme such as EIS, which I mentioned earlier in the book and which is described more fully in Appendix VI, you have to hold your shares for at least three years or you will forfeit your right to the tax breaks – which might mean you have to pay back to the taxman any income or capital gains tax breaks you previously received.

Another aspect of being an EIS investor is that you will have a number of forms to sign so you can claim your tax breaks from the taxman. You also have to record on your annual tax return the details of the companies you have invested in.

There are now signs that some platforms are beginning to see the value of setting up secondary market facilities to enable equity and even debt investors to sell their shares or loans to other investors. One example that is getting off the ground in the UK is www.liquity.com; another is www.secondmarket.com. Platforms such as www.syndicateroom.com and www.angellist.co are also prime candidates in my view for opening the route to easy sales of investments to other investors in the future.

Returns aside, as an equity investor you can expect to be kept informed about how the company you have invested in is doing. There should be fairly regular shareholder reports (at least once a year) and you should be entitled to receive the company's accounts. The best companies will maintain an active dialogue with their shareholders, often via a password-protected area of their website.

Depending on the terms you agreed when you made the investment, you may be entitled to rewards, extra access to the company's management team, invitations to shareholder days and more. For a few investors, you may even become involved with the company's management team, helping them to get the business trading and then growing successfully. However, remember that if you do get involved you need to clarify very clearly what your role is going to be. Are you a director of the company (which carries a lot of legal responsibilities with it), an employee or a paid consultant, or just someone giving some free mentoring support?

Whatever role you take up, you should make sure that you have all the arrangements set out in writing and, if money is exchanging hands, you should ensure you have proper contracts in place that set out everything very clearly.

There can be other financial rewards before the exit comes. Seedrs pays you 5% cash back on any money invested by friends, family and contacts you introduce to the platform. Interestingly, Seedrs has also recently introduced a special club for its largest investors called the Leedrs Club. You are automatically invited into the Leedrs Club if you are one of the top 10% of investors in the previous month, and you get to stay in the club until you end up in the bottom 25% of investors for a three-month period. Leedrs members get exclusive perks offered by the platform operator.

The equity fundraising world is also developing similar characteristics to the business angel and venture capital worlds, namely that a company once it has raised money is very likely indeed to come back to you to seek more investment. Typically, they need more money for one of two reasons: either the plan takes longer to develop and/or is more costly than the founders expected, so they need more money to see them through; or it starts going much better than planned and therefore more money is needed to exploit the potential that has been created. Whichever happens, do not be surprised if the founders come back to you sooner rather than later for more funding. The approach may be direct or via the launch of a new crowd funding campaign.

Remember that investing is not necessarily free. In the case of Seedrs, you will pay 7.5% of any profits you make on your investment when you exit.

When the exit does come, it is not necessarily going to be straight-forward. Not all exits are for cash. Sometimes you may be offered shares in the company that is buying the one you have invested in, or you may be offered loan stock in the buyer and they will then pay you what you are owed in line with the loan stock agreement. Whichever the result, you will have to sign a document where you agree to sell your shares for the money or other consideration being offered.

If an investment fails, it is most likely that the directors will put it into the hands of an administrator. They will then write to you and your fellow shareholders explaining what has happened and what will happen next. You will be invited to a creditors' meeting where everything will be explained to you, including how much money you may receive, although it is highly unlikely that you will receive anything. A few weeks later you will get a final letter explaining the final arrangements for the winding up of the company. At that point, if you have invested under EIS or SEIS you can claim some money back from HMRC under the loss relief provisions of the schemes.

Investors' views

One reason why investors like equity crowd funding is that it fills the funding gap for companies that cannot raise money elsewhere. They also like being influential. When I surveyed investors, they also spoke about their liking for platforms that provide services to the investor, such as post-investment deal management, and also they liked sites where the whole transaction could be completed online.

Here is one of the comments an investor made in the survey:

> *"[I like] equity crowd funding as it bridges the large funding gap that exists for start-up and early stage businesses."*

Another investor said:

> *"[I like] equity or equity-related [funding] – I feel it is important to have some kind of direct (or indirect) influence on the running of the company."*

But not everyone was a fan of equity crowd funding, as we've seen earlier in the book:

> *"Equity is pointless as there is generally no exit in sight and being part of a huge number of shareholders is problematic."*

Another person thought that trying to bring the traditional rules of investment into the crowd world is a bad idea:

> "I need to be close to the deal and fully understand it. I'm definitely not for parcelled deals designed to emulate a balanced portfolio. I guess I don't see the point in using innovative-ish tools to follow the herd."

And others worry about the future of equity crowd funding from an investor's perspective:

> "[With] equity-preference shares, when further rounds of investment are required, politics around preference status can get quite messy. Particularly if further investment needs have not been taken into account."

Social enterprise platforms

Platforms with a social ethos are very exciting for a funder. You can expect to receive news not only on how the project is proceeding but also on the underlying beneficiaries of the project. You may be offered the opportunity to visit the project too.

Investors' views

One of the key reasons why funders like social enterprise investing is because of the feel-good factor. As one investor told me:

> "[I like] social enterprises. This is an area that really benefits from crowd funding as it appeals to a wider part of the community."

When things go wrong

With any luck your crowd investing experience will always veer from satisfactory to absolutely delightful, but sadly things can go wrong.

Projects do fail for genuine reasons and businesses can fail because something happens that is beyond the management team's control. In these cases, your best bet is to take your loss on the chin and learn from the experience. After all, if there had been no excitement (aka risk!), you probably would not have got involved in the first place.

There are times, though, when you either suspect or know that you have been defrauded of your money. This is why it is very important to have done your homework before you start investing, as you need to know to whom you should turn if something has gone wrong. In some cases the platform operator may give you reasonable assistance to help you recover what you are owed, but it is extremely unlikely that they will admit any legal liability to you for any money or anything else you have lost, unless they have been knowingly negligent or otherwise at fault. It may be very expensive to prove that they were! It is always worth double-checking that the platforms you are using are properly regulated and insured before you do any business on them.

It is most likely that you will have to turn to the people who received your money for redress and probably pursue them through the courts to get your money back. This can be expensive and time-consuming and is also emotionally very damaging. As a rule, your best defence against fraud is to make sure that you can afford to lose what you have invested even if it was taken from you illegally.

There is one thing worth thinking about, though, especially if you are investing small sums: why don't you ring your credit card company and check to see if you would be covered, and under what terms, by their standard compensation arrangements if you use your card to pledge or invest? If they do agree that you are covered, if things go wrong you would then be entitled to seek redress through them.

Using the crowd to fight your battles

When things go wrong, it is very tempting to use the power of the crowd to try to help you win your fight. I would be very careful before you go down this route and you should certainly take some specialist advice from a litigation lawyer before you take any action. If you act without taking advice, you risk breaking the laws of defamation, libel and even conspiracy to pervert the course of justice. The penalties for you in these cases could be far worse than your original loss.

Crowds are powerful beasts. What you do to someone in the crowd can easily come back to haunt you. If you whip up the crowd into hostility against someone else, you should be aware that someone else might just do the same to you.

Conclusion

At the end of the day, the decisions you make about getting involved after you have invested will be personal to you. My main piece of advice is that you stay inside your comfort zone and don't promise what you cannot deliver. If you fail to do that, you might find that your crowd relationships get sticky. And, once again, never invest what you cannot afford to lose.

In summary

1. If you make a donation, take your reward in the form of the satisfaction you feel about helping someone else achieve their dreams, but don't place emotional baggage on the recipient along with your money.

2. If you do pledge funding, you have a right to expect the funders to use your money in the way they promised and you have a reasonable right to receive the reward you were promised. However, be aware that new projects carry intrinsic risks; sometimes they will fail and you will see neither your money back nor your reward. Stay engaged so you do not get any nasty surprises.

3. For debt funding, you are legally entitled to receive both interest payments and capital repayments. Remember that you will have to pay tax on your interest income. You may not be very engaged with the recipient of your money.

4. In equity you are buying shares for money. You therefore become a part-owner of that company and should be treated accordingly. Stay engaged and expect to be asked to invest again at least once if not several times.

5. If you are an equity investor and things go wrong, expect the administrator or receiver to write to you telling you

the state of play. If things go right, expect to receive a big cheque one day or to see your shares listed on a stock exchange.

6. When it comes to social enterprise investing, remember that your returns will be a mix of financial and social rewards. Don't muddle the two up. You will be very warmly received if you stay engaged with and supportive of the social campaigns you have backed.

7. Accept that, like any other sort of project or investment, things in the crowd can go wrong.

8. Before you get angry, always consider whether it is really worth having a fight with someone – as the emotional costs of the battle can be greater than the value of the money you lose.

9. Always read the small print before you invest so you know who to turn to if things go wrong.

10. Beware of trying to use the crowd to fight your battles – they might just turn on you.

Chapter 12

The future of crowd funding

My father-in-law, William Rees-Mogg, sadly died while I was writing this book. He was a great man and a better journalist. One of his mantras was that it was not his job to be right, but to be interesting. When it comes to writing a handbook like this, it needs to be both right and interesting for all the practical stuff. Up to this point, this is what I have endeavoured to do. But to add a bit of spice to conclude it, I thought you might enjoy reading about some of my thoughts on the future of crowd funding. I hope they will fit with William's requirement to be interesting; only time will tell whether they are right!

What will the rules of crowd funding be in years to come?

The rules around crowd funding are turning on a pinhead at the moment. If I had finished this book by its original deadline of 30th November 2012, it would have been full of optimism about the lead the US had taken with its JOBS Act, which effectively legalised crowd funding and placed it within the regulated world as governed by the SEC. In the UK and elsewhere, governments were trumpeting the advantages of most if not all crowd funding routes, especially debt funding. In the case of the UK, the government was actually going so far as to commit to spending in the market. But at the beginning of 2013, the SEC delayed the JOBS Act and is implementing it much more slowly than originally anticipated. While those in the US watch and wait, here in the UK, there is a big move by both debt and equity crowd platforms into compliance with more traditional regulatory structures, broadly speaking. For example, Crowdcube has not only obtained FCA regulation, but has even arranged for its investors to be protected by the Financial Services Compensation Scheme.

If I try to look forward into the late 2010s, on balance I think that the regulators' desire to protect us from the bad and the wicked will probably win, but that they will have created a new framework that will reflect the fact that the crowd will be able to find out, reveal and punish the bad and the wicked far quicker than the authorities. I hope that the new regulatory framework is simple to operate and focused on ensuring an orderly market for crowd funding, rather than simply being an exercise in business prevention.

Who will be in the crowd in five years' time?

In five years' time, I think there will be dozens and dozens of crowd platforms, but within 10 years I suspect that there will have been a period of consolidation — many platforms will have been bought out by their competitors or traditional financial services companies such as banks, or by the giants of the internet such as Google or Amazon.

It is telling that the UK government is already part of the crowd. It has been directly lending money to the various debt and alternative debt platforms since early 2013. Assuming its experience is successful at helping to stimulate lending to kick-start the UK's economic recovery and that the platform operators can make money, it would not surprise me if we see other governments following suit.

When it comes to investors, I believe that we are already seeing what will happen. Institutional investors will come to see parts, if not all, of the crowd funding platforms as an asset class — indeed, they are already getting involved in less risky platforms such as invoice auction sites (e.g. MarketInvoice). Meanwhile, the banks who are already reacting to the threats of the crowd will not only get their own acts together when it comes to traditional lending, but will also start providing finance via

Checked out item summary for
KWEH, MICHAEL S.N
16-08-2016 6:29PM

BARCODE: SN000000377900
LOCATION: scanf
TITLE: Crowd funding : how to raise more
DUE DATE: 06-09-2016

peer-to-peer lending – not just on Zopa, as they do already, either by providing money to third party debt platforms, but possibly within their own base of customers – arranging for their private customers to lend to their corporate customers perhaps or vice versa?

They will probably sit comfortably alongside everyone, from private funders investing under £500 a year to the super-wealthy who will put £1m or more to work at a time.

Will the industry consolidate or fracture further?

I think that today it is anyone's guess as to whether the early monsters in the crowd world, such as Kickstarter, will become pre-eminent in their space across the globe and start buying up or squashing smaller competitors, or whether the crowd will take on the characteristics of the financial services industry and thrive on having a multitude of different players in the market.

If I had to place a bet myself, I would opt for the latter case being the one that wins – at the end of the day, the crowd is all about finance, not about selling a branded physical product. What I cannot yet envisage is whether there will be dozens of competitors in each sub-segment of the crowd. I suspect that there will probably end up being two strong players and a small group of smaller niche platforms in each area.

What businesses will be raising money via the crowd?

This is where I get very excited. I am waiting for a Fortune 500 company to test-launch a new product via the crowd or a serious business with a £20m-plus turnover or even a quoted company raising crowd equity. I am certain that hundreds if not thousands of very established and respectable companies will be turning to crowd debt to fund themselves sooner rather than later.

How quickly will businesses be able to raise money?

I now have no doubt that crowd funding's biggest impact on fundraising will be the speed with which fundraising can be completed. There are now examples of businesses on all types of platform raising all of if not more than the money they need in a couple of days. You can see what I mean from the story of *Veronica Mars* below.

Case study

Veronica Mars

Veronica Mars was an American television series created by Rob Thomas that aired between 2004 and 2007 in three series. After the series ended, fans were calling out for a movie – Thomas was up for it as was star Kristen Bell. Warner Bros., however, weren't convinced that the fans wanted a film so put the idea on hold. Flash forward to 2013 and Rob Thomas announced that a Veronica Mars *movie was being made, financed by the fans through Kickstarter. In its first day on Kickstarter, the project broke records as the fastest project to reach first $1m, then $2m; the highest minimal pledging goal achieved; and the largest successful film project on Kickstarter. Over 91,500 people donated $5.7m – almost trebling the $2m target. Rewards included a copy of the film on DVD, a T-shirt, signed posters and, for the more generous backers, tickets to the premiere and after-party and a speaking role in the film itself. These rewards, which go further than the usual merchandise – hiring out a theatre for a private film screening for you and your friends, a voicemail message recorded by the stars, a walk-on part in the film – all make the donation seem more worthwhile. Not only is it allowing the fans to make the movie happen, but it is also including them in the project itself. Before launching the campaign, Warner Bros. were approached with the idea and have agreed to make and distribute the film if they receive the funding. Their $2m goal was reached in the first 10 hours of the campaign.*

Here in the UK, we have started to see how much crowd funding enables speedy fundraising. The main debt and alternative debt platforms pride themselves on arranging funding within a couple of days of the campaign going live, and in spring 2013 Crowdcube announced that it had completed an equity fundraising in just 2.5 days. I expect, if anything, fundraisings in the crowd to get quicker and quicker, especially as fundraisers get better at making their campaigns excellent and succinct and as funders get more used to finding and funding exactly the ones they want.

How will large companies react to the growth of crowd funding?

As you can see from the story of *Veronica Mars*, in the film world the big movie-makers are already working out ways to engage in the crowd funding phenomenon. Forward-thinking companies are partnering with relevant platforms – Procter & Gamble's partnership with CircleUp is a case in point. With the competitive threat created by crowd-supported businesses enabling start-ups to gather not only considerable sums of money but also, and perhaps even more importantly, tens of thousands of customers in just a few weeks, large companies will no longer be able to use their might to slow down their new competitors. Indeed, it would not surprise me if the large companies start using the crowd to launch their own new products in the future. I also expect to see a lot of large companies moving in with attempts to buy fast-growing crowd platforms, especially the debt ones.

How will the platforms innovate?

Platform operators are innovating all the time. ThinCats' secondary market was launched in January 2013 as a way of transferring loans between members at the value of the remaining capital balance. There is absolutely no doubt at all that other platforms will continue to do things that will make the market better and much more efficient. It will also become more and more liquid. It would not surprise me to see a crowd platform becoming large enough to swallow some of the world's most established stock and other markets. We will see crowd funding reach into many areas that have been off-limits for most private investors for decades, such as the commodities markets, the metals markets and even sectors such as shipping. I predict that the next big crowd platform will offer crowd-based insurance funding. And in a sense we will have just come full circle, back to the days when Lloyds insurance was financed by private investors. The differences will be that the opportunities will be bigger, the market will be more transparent, and many, many more people will be involved.

Will there be a big scandal?

I have no doubt that there will be scandals in the crowd and that they will make headlines. Where and when one will come I cannot possibly predict, but the sheer size of the crowd and the fact that larger and larger sums of money are in play inevitably mean that criminally minded people will get involved. Sadly, there will be some who get away with it, but I am just as certain that the majority will be found out. Their crimes will be more traceable and they will be brought to justice. And, with any luck, once the criminals have been exposed, the crowd and the authorities will make it their mission to ensure that they do not get away with it a second time.

Conclusion

I wonder what you predict will happen in the crowd. While writing this book I have become more and more inspired by the potential that crowd funding offers both to people who need money and to those who have it and want to put it to good use. Even in the last couple of months, I have heard of and sometimes met with several amazing entrepreneurs who are getting their crowd platforms up and running. There will be more next month, too.

The big challenges that face crowd funding, such as regulation, are being addressed, if not yet completely resolved; platform operators and users are innovating all the time; and, thanks to them, the world really is a better place.

I hope that after reading this book, you too are going to join the crowd – but you'll be better engaged and have more understanding than anyone who has not read it!

Appendices

Appendix I
Glossary of terms

I have taken these key terms from my website www.angelnews.co.uk. They are all terms you should familiarise yourself with if you are going to raise capital from investors, especially through equity and debt. However, they are terms used in all types of fundraising and are just as applicable when it comes to crowd funding.

"A" round
A financing event whereby venture capitalists invest in a company that was previously financed by founders and/or angels. The "A" is from series "A" preferred stock. See also "B" round.

Accredited investor, also known as a certificated investor
A term used in both the US and the UK to refer to investors who have been accredited as wealthy enough to invest in high-risk investments – the definition of which is defined in law in each jurisdiction. In the UK, there are certificated high net worth investors and certificated sophisticated investors. In the US, certificated high net worth investors have to have free investable assets (excluding their main home) in excess of $1m. In the UK, such investors have to have free investable assets of £250,000 or more (excluding their main home, insurances and pensions) or to have an income in excess of £100,000 a year.

"B" round
A financing event in an unquoted company whereby investors such as venture capitalists are sufficiently interested in a company to provide additional funds after the "A" round of financing. Typically, new investors are invited to join existing shareholders in such a round of financing. Any later rounds are called "C", "D", and so on.

Break-even
The level of sales necessary for a company to cover all its fixed and variable costs. Above break-even sales, a company will be profitable. Break-even can be expressed over any time period and in terms of units or value of sales.

Business angel
An individual who invests capital in a small business, and who will often be actively involved in helping the business to grow.

Business angel networks
Private or public sector owned and operated networks where business angels can see private equity investment opportunities and decide whether to opt in to an investment. Such networks also enable angels to syndicate investments. Many networks in the UK operate small venture capital funds that can invest alongside angels in the network. Often these funds have been invested by private investors or angels in the network. Typically, networks do not act in a corporate finance or other advisory role.

Capital gains
The difference between the price paid for shares (or other capital assets) and the price at which they are sold.

Cash flow
The flow of cash in and out of a company. A company may be profitable but still have a negative cash flow and therefore fail. A company may be loss-making and, for a time, still have a positive cash flow. First-time entrepreneurs should take care to understand the distinction between profit and loss and cash flow.

Co-investment/syndication
When a group of investors invests alongside one another in an investee company. Frequently this includes individuals (usually general partners) alongside a private equity fund in a financing round.

Convertible bonds
A formal loan instrument used to record the money a company has borrowed and the terms of borrowing, e.g. the interest rate, the date

it will be redeemed and the dates on which interest will be paid. The instrument also defines the terms on which the loan can be converted into equity shares, including how the conversion will be calculated and the dates on which it can be converted.

Corporation tax
The tax on company profits.

Current assets
Assets that can be converted into cash within 12 months or used in the same period to pay a company's liabilities. Typically, current assets will include stock waiting to be sold and debtors who are due to pay their bills within 12 months. See also fixed assets.

Development capital/expansion capital/growth capital
This usually refers to equity capital raised to provide for the company to grow ambitiously.

Dilution
When an existing shareholder sees their percentage shareholding reduced by the issuing of new shares. This can take place due to the conversion of other instruments into the class of shares or by a new financing round.

Dilution protection
This is a provision frequently demanded by venture capitalists and mainly applies to ordinary and convertible shares. It involves the issue of more ordinary and convertible shares for no cash to the shareholder in a later funding round in order to ensure that these shareholders retain the same percentage of the company that they held before the fundraising. Sometimes it is effected by existing shares being split in an appropriate ratio to have the same impact. Shareholders' agreements also typically contain anti-dilution provisions in the event of a down round (q.v.) financing later on at a lower valuation than the one at which they invested.

Dividends
Once a company is profitable is it able to declare that some or all of its profits should be paid out to its shareholders. Such payments are known as dividends.

Down round
A down round is when a later fundraising takes place that values the shares already in issue before the fundraising at a lower price than the price that investors originally paid for them.

Drag-along rights/pull-along rights
A majority shareholder's right, obligating shareholders whose shares are bound into the shareholders' agreement to sell their shares into an offer the majority wishes to execute. See also tag-along rights.

Dual entry
Dual or double entry book keeping is fundamental to accounting. It is based on the idea that all financial movements have an equal and opposite effect in different places in the accounts. So a debt in one account will be offset by a credit in another account. All the credits must equal all the debts. If they do not, the accounts are not correct.

Due diligence
This is when potential investors analyse and assess the desirability, value and potential of an investment opportunity. This can vary from a relatively light-handed procedure to an extensive exercise taking months. It is frequently a cause of the great length of time it can take to complete a financing round.

Early stage
When a company that has completed its seed stage and its start-up stage has a core management team, has proven its concept or completed its beta test, has achieved some sales, but is not yet profitable or cash flow positive. See also seed stage.

Earnings before interest, taxes, depreciation and amortisation (EBITDA)
This is used as a measure of cash flow, as it adjusts for non-cash items in the profit and loss account and also tax. It also indicates what funds a company might have available to fund loan payments on borrowings.

Earnings per share (EPS)
The net profit divided by the number of ordinary shares in issue. Fully diluted earnings per share is calculated as the net profit divided by the

total number of shares that would be in issue if all the shares in share option plans etc. were exercised.

Elevator pitch

A very short (five-minute) presentation of an entrepreneur's idea, business model and case and details of their competitive position delivered to potential investors.

Enterprise Investment Scheme (EIS)

The EIS was launched in January 1994 and aims to encourage wealthy individuals to invest in smaller, unquoted companies and to play an active part in their management, thereby becoming business angels (q.v.). An EIS investor receives capital gains tax and income tax relief at varying levels provided the shares that are held under EIS are owned for three years. If the investment fails, further tax relief is available. Under the EIS a business angel investor may be paid a reasonable salary by the investee company and may become a director, but must not have been previously involved with the company before investing. There are restrictions on which types of company are eligible under EIS. If a company obtains a quotation on the main market of the London Stock Exchange within the qualifying period for EIS tax relief, the investor loses those reliefs, but the company can list on the AIM and Sharemark markets without losing the relief.

Enterprise value (EV)

This is a more "true" measure of a company's value, as it includes the debt and quasi-debt that an acquirer would have to take on when buying a company as well as market capitalisation. It also adjusts for cash and cash equivalents that an acquirer would have access to if it controlled the company.

Entrepreneur

Normally an owner of an independent business and a term used to describe an enterprising person, and therefore often related to the setting up of a new or growing company. Business owners who have no ambitions to grow their business beyond a level that gives them a secure income would not be described as entrepreneurs. Entrepreneurs are also typically those who are seeking venture capital.

Equity
Equity or share capital is the risk capital provided to finance a business. If the business fails, the equity will usually be lost. If the business succeeds, the profits belong to the shareholders.

Exit route/exit strategy
The method for liquidating an investment in a company while obtaining the maximum possible return. Exit strategies can include selling or distributing the investee company's shares in and after an initial public offering (IPO), a sale of the investee to another company, or a recapitalisation. Increasingly, venture capitalists are considering selling in the secondary market (q.v.) as other exit opportunities are limited.

Factoring
A company goes to a factor to discount its invoices, with the factor paying a percentage of the value of the invoice upfront and the balance, minus a fee, when the invoice is finally paid by the creditor. A similar exercise is called invoice discounting, when the company manages its own sales ledger and debt collection rather than the factoring agency doing so.

Family Office
A Family Office is a private company that manages investments and trusts for a single wealthy family. Sometimes one organisation acts as a Family Office for several wealthy families.

Financial Conduct Authority (FCA)
The immensely powerful UK regulator of the financial services industry. It is often referred to as "the Regulator" and has recently replaced the Financial Services Authority.

Fixed assets
Assets such as land and buildings that are fixed and cannot be moved or sold easily or quickly. See also current assets.

Free cash flow
The cash flow of a company available to service the capital structure of the firm. It is typically measured as operating cash flow less capital expenditures and tax obligations.

Friends and family shares

Shares to friends and family members issued early on in the life of a company. Usually these shares are issued at a heavily discounted rate compared with the price achieved at an eventual IPO.

Fund of funds

A specialist fund set up to invest in a range of private equity fund managers, who in turn invest the capital into investee companies. It is used as a method by investors to spread risk across a wider private equity portfolio than would otherwise be achievable.

Gearing

The ratio of debt to equity in a company. In general, the higher the gearing, the higher the percentage of annual profits that must be used to, pay interest and the greater the vulnerability of the company to events outside its control, such as a rise in interest rates or a fall in sales. There is no precise and accepted definition of gearing and therefore the way the figure is calculated should be checked. Grey areas can be long-term loans from shareholders and convertible equity.

General partner

The general partner is responsible for all management decisions of a limited partnership. The general partner has a legal duty to act in the best interests of the limited partners (q.v.) and is fully liable for the organisation's actions.

Hockey stick projections

The general shape and form of a chart showing the financial and associated projections that increase dramatically at some point in the future. Frequently used as a derogative term to describe the over-optimistic projections prepared by entrepreneurs.

Indemnities

The promise that, if warranties (q.v.) made by a warrantor are proved to be false, then compensation will be paid to the people to whom the warranty has been addressed.

Initial public offering (IPO)/flotation

This is when a company lists its shares for the first time on a stock market such as the main list of the London Stock Exchange, AIM or, in the US, NASDAQ.

Intellectual property

A company's intangible assets, including patents, brand names, etc.

Internal rate of return (IRR)

A measure of financial performance – the rate at which the present value of one or more investments is equal to the present value of the returns on those investments.

Invoice discounting

A variation of factoring (q.v.).

Lead investor

The angel or venture capitalist who leads the fundraising and leads the shareholders once the investment round is completed. Usually, although not always, they will be the largest investor in the company.

Leasing

Payment for an asset by regular payments over a fixed period, with ownership of the asset held by the lessor. Depending on the terms of the lease, the asset can be retained by the lessor or acquired by the lessee. Can be an off-balance sheet method of financing and therefore not readily identifiable by third parties, although it has a significant effect on gearing (q.v.).

Lemon

A bad investment. "Lemons ripen before plums."

Limited partner (LP)

An investor in a limited partnership who has no voice in the management of the partnership, has limited liability and has priority over general partners in the liquidation of a partnership.

Limited partnership

A partnership comprised of a general partner and limited partners. The general partner receives a management fee and a percentage of the profits (or carried interest). The limited partners receive income, capital gains and tax benefits.

Liquidation
The sale of all of a company's assets, for distribution to creditors and shareholders in order of priority.

Liquidation preference
The contractual right of an investor to priority in receiving the proceeds from the liquidation of a company. For example, two times liquidation preference equates to the right to receive two times the original investment upon liquidation.

Liquidity event
When an investor realises a gain or loss on an investment and ends their relationship with an investee company.

Listing
When a company trades its shares on a stock market.

Loan capital
A form of debt that has to be repaid at a specified time in the future (as distinct from a bank overdraft that may be called in at short notice).

Lock-up
The period of time during which certain shareholders waive their rights to sell their shares and are physically prevented from selling after the flotation of a company. Underwriters to a flotation generally insist upon lock-ups of at least 180 days from shareholders with 1% ownership or more in order to allow an orderly market to develop in the shares. The management and directors of the company and strategic partners are also usually subject to a lock-up.

Mezzanine financing

1. Financing for a company immediately prior to its IPO. Mezzanine-level financing can be in the form of preference shares (q.v.), convertible bonds (q.v.) or subordinated debt (q.v.).
2. A financing instrument that has elements of both debt and equity, e.g. convertible debt.

Net asset value (NAV)
The assets or investments in the company or fund divided by the outstanding number of shares of the company or fund.

Net present value (NPV)
The sum of the cash flows of a project or investment, including the initial cash investment and final cash realised on exit, discounted to come to a present value of those cash flows.

Newco
A generic name for any new company.

Non-disclosure agreement (NDA)
The agreement issued by entrepreneurs to potential investors to protect the privacy of their ideas when disclosing those ideas to third parties.

Non-executive director (NED)
"Part-time" directors who share all the legal responsibilities of their executive colleagues on the board of a company. The general view is that they can operate as an independent director able to take a long-term view of a company and protect the interests of shareholders. An investor will often appoint a non-executive to the board of an investee company as one way of monitoring their investment.

Observation rights
The right taken by non-management shareholders to attend and observe, but not actively participate in, a company's board meetings. See also shadow director.

Option pool
The number of shares set aside for future issue to employees of a private company.

Pari passu
Equal to.

Participating preferred shares
Shares that bear the right to a stated dividend (and frequently a return of the original investment upon flotation or sale of the company)

and also to additional dividends related to payments of dividends to ordinary shareholders.

Partnership
An entity in which each partner shares in its profits, losses and liabilities. The entity itself is not taxed. Instead, each partner is responsible for the taxes on their share of the profits and losses.

Plum
A successful investment. "Plums ripen later than lemons."

Poison pill
A right issued by a corporation as a preventative anti-takeover measure enabling a party to purchase shares in either their company or in the combined target and bidder entity at a substantial discount, usually 50%. This discount may make the takeover prohibitively expensive. This is common in the US.

Portfolio companies
The companies in which a venture capital fund is invested.

Post-money valuation
This is the valuation of the company immediately after a round of financing. It comprises the enterprise value (q.v.) of the company and the amount of cash invested in the round. For example, a venture capitalist may invest £3m in a company valued at £2m "pre-money" (before the investment was made). As a result, the start-up will have a post-money valuation of £5m.

Pre-emption right
A shareholder's right to acquire shares in the future when a new round of financing is held, thereby preventing that shareholder from being diluted.

Pre-money valuation
The valuation of a company prior to a round of investment. This valuation is calculated using various methods, such as discounted price earnings ratios multiplied by historical, current or future earnings, or an NPV computation. It can also be calculated based on the valuations of comparable quoted companies and on the valuations achieved in previous exits of comparable private companies.

Preference shares/preferred shares
A class of shares that may pay dividends at a specified rate and that has priority over common stock in the payment of dividends and the liquidation of assets.

Preferred dividend
A dividend accruing on preferred shares.

Price earnings ratio (PER or P/E)
The quoted market price per share divided by earnings per share, or, alternatively, market capitalisation divided by net profit after tax. Used by analysts as an indicator of the expected future performance of a company relative to its peers.

Private equity
Shares in a company that is not listed on a public exchange. Such shares are generally illiquid and thought of as a long-term investment. As they are not listed on an exchange, any investor wishing to sell their shares must find a buyer in the absence of a marketplace, and there are often restrictions on their ability to transfer these shares under the terms of the shareholders' agreement.

Private placement memorandum/investment memorandum
The document supplied by a company and often prepared with the support of expert advisers such as corporate financiers and lawyers which details the fundraising. In many ways it is similar to a business plan used to fundraise from private investors.

Ratchet/sliding scale
The basis for offering increased equity interest in a company to its management, based on the results of the company.

Recapitalisation
The reorganisation of a company's capital structure.

Receivership
The common term for administrative receivership, which is when a company's directors are no longer able to manage the company

themselves and vote to transfer administration of the company to specialist receivers, who manage the business in order to meet the costs of paying off creditors to the company (including the taxman, lenders, suppliers who are owed money and, finally, shareholders). Going into receivership does not inevitably mean that the company will fail, as receivers will usually first try to find a buyer for the business as a going concern (i.e. while it keeps trading). There are lots of legal procedures and processes relating to going into receivership, which include an investigation into the directors who have passed the company into receivership.

Redeemable preferred shares/exploding preferred shares
Shares that are redeemable (i.e. bought back by the company) at the shareholder's option after (typically) five years, which in turn gives the shareholders (potentially converting to creditors) leverage to induce the company to arrange a liquidity event.

Restructure
This usually involves major changes in the organisation of a company, possibly by changing the management and/or the share ownership structure.

Return on capital employed (ROCE)
Here is the calculation for ROCE:

$$\text{ROCE} = \text{earnings before interest and tax (EBIT)} / (\text{capital employed} + \text{short-term borrowings} - \text{intangible assets})$$

ROCE provides an idea of the efficiency and profitability of a company's capital investments. Return on average capital employed (ROACE) can also be calculated; this takes the average of opening and closing capital employed for the time period and gives a more measured result, adjusting for movements in the company's assets over time.

Rights issue/offer
This is when a company offers new shares to existing shareholders, usually at a discount off the market price. Shareholders who do not

exercise these rights are usually diluted by the offering. Rights are often transferable, allowing the holder to sell them on the open market to others who may wish to exercise them.

Risk/risk factors

Investors accept risks when they invest. The principal risk is that they lose money on their investment. This can be due to inflation, interest rates, default, politics, foreign exchange, call provisions, etc. In private equity, the risks that the investors are likely to face are included in the risk factors section of the private placement memorandum (q.v.).

Road show

This is when a company makes a series of presentations to potential investors to tell them about their business and to invite them to invest. It is also known as a "dog and pony show". The company will usually be accompanied by its financial advisers.

Roll-over relief

Tax relief, or more precisely tax deferral, on capital gains that is granted if the gains are reinvested in a suitable vehicle, e.g. an EIS qualifying company.

Run rate

1. How the financial performance of a company would look if you were to extrapolate current results over a certain period of time. The run rate helps to put the company's latest results in perspective. For example, if a company has revenues of £100m in its latest quarter, the CEO might say: "Our latest quarter puts us at a £400m run rate." All this is saying is that if the company were to perform at the same level for the next year, they'd have annual revenues of £400m. The run rate can be a very deceptive number, especially in seasonal industries. A great example of this is a retailer after Christmas. Almost all retailers experience higher sales during the holiday season. It is very unlikely that the coming quarters will have sales as strong as those in the fourth quarter, and so the run rate will likely overstate next year's revenue.

2. The average annual dilution from company stock option grants over the most recent three-year period recorded in the annual report.

Secondary market

1. The market for the sale of partnership interests in private equity funds. Sometimes limited partners choose to sell their interest in a partnership, typically to raise cash or because they cannot meet their obligation to invest more capital according to the takedown schedule. Certain investment companies specialise in buying these partnership interests at a discount.
2. The term used to describe the trading of shares in a company after its flotation on a stock market.

Seed stage/seed capital
The first round of capital for a start-up business. Seed money usually takes the structure of a loan or an investment in preferred stock or convertible bonds, although sometimes it is common stock. Seed money provides start-up companies with the capital required for their initial development and growth. Angel investors and early stage venture capital funds often provide seed money.

Seed stage financing
An initial stage of a company's growth characterised by establishing a management team, business plan development, prototype development and beta testing.

Senior debt
The element of a financial package that consists of bank lending. It is called "senior" because if things go wrong, the lender has higher priority than those who provided mezzanine (q.v.) or equity finance.

Shadow director
A person who, although they are not legally a director of a company, is deemed to play the de facto role of a director in that company, e.g. they have sufficient influence over decisions made by the company. This can

be a significant issue for large shareholders in a company who may not wish to have a board seat, but can find themselves responsible for a company's actions if they have been involved in running the company or influencing how it is run.

Share option/stock options
The right to purchase or sell a share at a specified price within a stated period. The transaction takes place between the existing shareholder and another party. Note: frequently the term "warrant" is used interchangeably with "option". Options are often used for employee incentives and compensation.

Silent partner
An investor who is not involved in the running or strategic direction of a company of which they are a shareholder.

Slippage
A delay experienced by a company in achieving financial projections as forecast by the company's plan.

Sole investor
See lead investor.

Sophisticated investor
An investor in high-risk assets (e.g. private equity) who has been approved by a specialist in the relevant field as being an expert in investing in that asset class. The term is defined in the Financial Services and Markets Act 2000. A sophisticated investor has less protection under the law than other types of investor, such as "ordinary" investors, who are often called "retail investors".

Spin-out
The emergence of a company in its own right from a larger entity, e.g. from a business or, more commonly in the UK, from a university research department.

Star
A high-growth company performing well.

Start-up capital
Capital that is raised after the seed capital stage to enable the company to commence trading.

Strategic investors
Investors who add value to a company by using their industry and personal ties.

Subordinated debt
A loan that ranks behind a company's other loans if that company becomes insolvent or goes into liquidation. It is repaid only after more senior debt (q.v.) has been repaid. Often, new investors will insist that existing loans made by investors will be subordinate to their own as one of the conditions of their funding.

Subscription agreement/shareholders' agreement
The agreement signed by investor, the company and its directors in a financing round, setting out the terms and conditions of the investment and obligations of the signatories to it.

Sweat equity
Equity that is given to the founder of the company in recognition of the effort (sweat) that they have expended in getting the company started.

Syndicate
Underwriters or brokers/dealers who sell a security as a group.

Tag-along rights/rights of co-sale
This is when a minority shareholder is given the right to include their shares in any sale of control and at the same price offered to the majority shareholders.

Takedown schedule
The schedule agreed between limited and general partners which states how much money the limited partners can demand from the general partners for new investments. Sometimes known as drawdown.

Term sheet
A summary of the terms the investor is prepared to accept. This is a non-binding outline of the principal points that the subscription agreement (q.v.) and related agreements will cover in detail.

Time value of money
The concept that all money can earn a cash return: therefore, £1 today will be worth more in the future if invested, after adjusting for inflation.

Trade sale
The sale of a company to another company. As a form of exit, it is an alternative to flotation and is more common.

Treasury stock
Redeemable stock issued by a company, but later reacquired. It may be held in the company's treasury indefinitely, reissued to the public, or retired. Treasury stock receives no dividends and does not carry voting power while held by the company.

Turnaround
An investment in a company in trouble that seeks to revive the company's fortunes and set it on a profitable course.

Venture capitalists
Capitalists who invest in unquoted companies, taking an equity percentage of around 25%. In some cases they offer managerial advice or support in return for a management fee.

Venture catalyst
Venture catalysts help speed up the process of a company raising investment by screening business plans.

Vintage year
The year a fund starts to make investments.

Vulture capital
A derogatory term used for venture capitalists by people who believe that venture capitalists take too much and offer too little when they invest.

Warrant/stock purchase warrant/subscription warrant

A type of security that entitles the holder to buy a proportionate amount of shares at a specified price at any time or at certain points for a period of years. Warrants are usually issued alongside another instruments, e.g. ordinary or preference shares (q.v.) or a bond to enhance the marketability of the accompanying securities.

Warranties

Assurances that are given by the selling shareholder or the directors of a company, verifying that statements they have made about the company and the state of the finances are true. See also indemnities.

Weighted average cost of capital (WACC)

A calculation of a firm's cost of capital that weights each category of capital proportionately. Included in the WACC calculation are all capital sources, including all types of shares and debt. WACC is calculated by multiplying the cost of each capital component by its proportional weighting and then adding them all up.

$$WACC = E/V \times Re + D/V \times Rd \times (1\text{-}Tc)$$
Where:
Re = cost of equity
Rd = cost of debt
E = market value of the firm's equity
D = market value of the firm's debt
$V = E + D$
E/V = percentage of financing that is equity
D/V = percentage of financing that is debt
Tc = corporate tax rate

WACC is the average of the cost of each of these sources of financing weighted by their respective usage in the given situation. A weighted average shows how much interest the company has to pay for every pound, euro or dollar it borrows from third parties, whether they are shareholders or debt providers. A firm's WACC is the overall required return on the business as a whole. It is the appropriate discount rate (q.v.) to use when calculating cash flows for the business. Source: www. investopoedia.com (edited).

White knight
An investor who rescues a company in distress. It can also be a bidder considered to be friendly to the interests of the management who is invited to bid for a company when the takeover target is facing a hostile bid.

Working capital
Capital that is used to finance the ordinary trading activities of a company, e.g. raw materials and labour costs, and to finance debtors or receivables. An accounting definition would be current assets minus current liabilities. Note: for start-up businesses, the working capital requirements can be larger than the requirements to acquire fixed assets. For some trading businesses, a rise in sales can lead to a disproportionate increase in working capital requirements.

Workout
A negotiated agreement between debtors and creditors outside the bankruptcy process.

Write-off
This is when an asset's value is written down to nil on the balance sheet and the write-off amount is taken as an expense through the profit and loss account. It is a non-cash item.

Write-up/write-down
An subjective upward or downward adjustment to the value of an asset on a balance sheet. In the case of a very large asset, a company may seek an independent valuation from an expert to justify their write-up/write-down to investors and third parties.

Appendix II

The history of crowd funding

By Jenny McLaren

Raising finance for a business by selling equity to multiple investors is nothing new. As far back as 12th-century France, people have been trading securities through banks. Italian companies were the first to issue what we now call shares, and this spread to England in the 16th century. This has evolved and grown into what is known as the global stock market. This has generally been the domain of wealthy private investors and institutional investors such as pension funds, although there have been occasions when there has been a spike in the number of small private investors, such as during the spate of privatisations undertaken by the Conservative government in the 1980s and 1990s. Crowd funding has now opened investment up to anyone and has made it easy for individual private investors to invest very small sums in the shares of a company, as well as to fund them by lending and other means.

In 1997, American fans raised $60,000 in donations to fund a US tour for British band Marillion. This was done independently of the band, who have since gone on to use this method to record and market three studio albums. Crowd funding is traditionally used to fund creative projects, and the first documented crowd funding website, ArtistShare (2000), was designed for music projects.

Brian Camelio founded ArtistShare as a way for fans to finance the production cost of an album that would be sold only online.

This developed into a completely new type of business model for creative artists. To date, ArtistShare projects have received 15 Grammy nominations and six Grammy wins. Since the first project in 2003, ArtistShare has been allowing fans to show appreciation for their favourite artists by funding their projects. In exchange, fans get access to the creative process, limited edition recordings, VIP access to events or recording sessions, and even credit listings on the final product.

One of the most successful and well known crowd funding sites is Kickstarter. Since its launch in April 2009, Kickstarter has helped raise over $735m from over 4.5 million people to fund more than 46,000 projects. The projects with the highest success rate fall within the music, film and video categories. Even with its headquarters in New York and the requirement that a US citizen be involved in each US project (and a UK citizen in a project on the UK site), Kickstarter receives funding from around the world by accepting all major card types through Amazon Payments.

Funding for creative projects usually comes from fans who have a vested interest in the project. From this interest, they help spread the word through social media. Kickstarter allows project owners to keep 100% ownership of the project. Other sites such as PledgeMusic raise funds by artists selling limited edition merchandise for various donation amounts. This method raises funds through exclusive purchases rather than donations. Kickstarter's main competitor is IndieGoGo.

One of the most phenomenally successful campaigns to have come from a crowd funding platform is the Pebble e-paper watch. After founder Eric Migicovsky failed to raise the necessary capital, he put the project on Kickstarter. He set his target at $100,000 for his watch that linked to the wearer's smartphone. Within two days in April 2012, he had reached 10 times that amount and raised a final total of $10,266,844. Over 69,000 individuals essentially pre-ordered their watch to help him reach that target. Since the campaign ended, another 15,000 people have gone on to buy a Pebble watch.

Of course, not every project that tries to use crowd funding is successful. Kickstarter reports only a 43% success rate, with 10,994 projects failing to raise any finance. This could be due to a number of factors, such as failing to engage with supporters or setting an unrealistic target. Companies that tend to use crowd funding will do so because they were considered too risky by banks and venture capitalists. Take the example of Eyez, high-tech glasses that promised to record live video. More than 2,000 people contributed over $300,000 to get their hands on a pair at the launch in autumn 2011. By autumn 2012, the backers were yet to receive their glasses and the company refused to answer questions or release product updates.

A lack of regulation post-fundraising can mean that using crowd funding as a business can be tricky. There are also laws around the world prohibiting private companies from soliciting funds from the public unless filed with a regulatory body – for example, the Financial Conduct Authority in the UK. Different platforms get around these issues in different ways. With some business sectors, such as biotechnology, issues of scale can be a problem when trying to use crowd funding as a method. Easier ways of crowd funding can be seen around the world with co-operative groups. With the rise of the internet, this idea spread as people were now able to reach volunteers all around the globe.

As of 2012, crowd funding platforms raised $2.7bn and funded over one million campaigns worldwide and shows no sign of slowing down. As of autumn 2012, Kickstarter allowed UK-based companies to join its platform, meaning that a whole new group of businesses is able to utilise this method of funding. Activists in the United States lobbied the government to make it legal for entrepreneurs to use crowd funding to raise limited capital at the early stages. This led to crowd funding receiving attention from policy makers, and it had a direct mention in the JOBS Act. This legislation – signed into law by President Obama in April 2012 – allows for fundraisings of up to $1m from a much wider group of smaller investors with few restrictions. Massolution forecasts an 81% increase in global crowd funding for 2013, bringing the total raised to $5.1bn. Lobby groups are also active in the United Kingdom to make this an accessible method for small businesses to raise finance.

Appendix III

Top crowd funding platforms

Top UK sites for equity crowd funding

Crowdcube
www.crowdcube.com
Fees: It is currently free to register – usually a £250 listing fee. Crowdcube deducts a success fee of 5% and legal fees of £1,750 If the target amount is raised
Most suitable for: Must be a limited company

Seedrs
www.seedrs.com
Fees: Free to join, but a 7.5% fee from the total amount you raise
Most suitable for: Start-ups

GrowthFunders
www.growthfunders.com
Fees: 5% plus legal fees
Most suitable for: Any business

SeedUps
www.seedups.com
Fees: Completion fee
Most suitable for: Start-ups

Grow VC
www.growvc.com
Fees: 2.5% of raised capital
Most suitable for: Start-ups

Bank to the Future
www.banktothefuture.com
Fees: 5% + company secretariat fee of £1,750+VAT if you meet funding goal; 10% if not
Most suitable for: Businesses wanting a variety of fundraising solutions in one place

Top UK sites for straight debt, peer-to-peer lending

ThinCats
www.thincats.com
Fees: Interest on loans
Most suitable for: Established businesses

Mayfair Bridging
www.mayfairbridging.com
Fees: Interest and 2% arrangement fee and c£800+VAT legal fees
Most suitable for: People with property

RateSetter
www.ratesetter.com
Fees: Loan and interest plus an administration fee and credit rate fee
Most suitable for: Creditworthy borrowers

Funding Circle
www.fundingcircle.com
Fees: Interest on loans plus a fee of 2%–5%
Most suitable for Anyone looking to borrow between £5,000 and £500,000

Rebuildingsociety
www.rebuildingsociety.com
Fees: 1.9%–4.9% fee plus interest on loans
Most suitable for: Any UK business which has:

- at least two years of filed accounts
- up-to-date management accounts
- no outstanding county court judgments

Top sites for alternative debt

MarketInvoice
http://marketinvoice.com
Fees: Pay-per-use
Most suitable for: Anyone with an outstanding invoice

BusinessFunding
www.businessfunding.co.uk
Fees: Sign-up fee
Most suitable for: Anyone

Platform Black
www.platformblack.com
Fees: Pay-per-use
Most suitable for: Anyone with an outstanding invoice

Top UK sites for pledge funding

Kickstarter
www.kickstarter.com
Fees: 5% fee to Kickstarter and 3% processing fee plus VAT
Most suitable for: Anyone

Crowdfunder
www.crowdfunder.co.uk
Fees: Free to join, then 5% commission on reaching your target
Most suitable for: Anyone

Fundable
www.fundable.com
Fees: $99 per month your pitch is active, 3.5% credit card
Most suitable for: Anyone

PledgeMusic
www.pledgemusic.com
Fees: 15% fee on successful projects
Most suitable for: Musicians

IndieGoGo
www.indiegogo.com
Fees: 4%–9% fee on successful projects plus a 3% card processing fee
(plus $25 for non-US projects)
Most suitable for: Anyone (not-for-profit organisations receive a 25%
reduction in site fees)

Top sites for social finance

CrowdMission
http://crowdmission.com
Fees: 5% fee if target is reached, plus legal fee of £1,750 if successful
Most suitable for: Social entrepreneurs

Buzzbnk
www.buzzbnk.org
Fees: £25 registration fee plus 5% fee on successful projects
Most suitable for: Social ventures

Spacehive
https://spacehive.com
Fees: Administration fees of 3.75% on the first £500,000, 2.5% on the
next £500,000 and 1.5% thereafter, plus transaction fees
Most suitable for: Public area regeneration projects

StartSomeGood
http://startsomegood.com
Fees: 5% plus PayPal fee of 2.9%
Most suitable for: Social entrepreneurs

Kiva
www.kiva.com
Fees: varying interest rates
Most suitable for: microfinance, particularly in developing countries

Appendix IV

Getting the financial underpinning of your crowd campaign right

By Johnny Martin FCA (www.johnnymartin.co.uk)

Investors know that behind every successful business are good business and financial systems. So your business plan needs to convey not only the excitement of your venture but also that you are a safe pair of hands who has a plan, knows how to execute it and has (or will have) enough resources to deliver. One of the most important things that investors will look for will be how competent you are at projecting what the likely sales and costs of the business will be.

The context of financial projections

The language of business is numbers. You have to have numbers in your business plan to show investors how profitable the business will become and, crucially, how much cash is required to deliver the plan. Investors need the numbers to assess the potential return they are likely to make from your investment and to assess whether this is sufficient given the level of *perceived* risk.

When it comes to the numbers there are three sets to think about: your historical numbers if you are already trading current trading (especially the cash you have available day to day) and the projections you prepare based on how you expect the future performance of your business to turn out. Each set of numbers should follow the same format and have the same headings, or you will get confused and you will confuse others. The financial rules or principles you use for each set of numbers should also be the same.

There are three main areas you need to cover in your numbers:

1. income and expenses shown in your profit and loss report
2. cash and cash flow – your cash flow numbers
3. keeping track of what the business owns (assets) and owes (liabilities) shown in your balance sheet.

As soon as you start trading, although it may be tempting to try to run the business numbers via a spreadsheet, I recommend that you use a good accounting software system, as it will help you to compile these reports easily and it will save you lots of time in the future. Using a software package will help you to generate financial reports and deal with tricky things such as making sure your balance sheet does what it should do, i.e. balance!

Accounting theory – the essential things to know

Profit is different from cash

Profit doesn't equal cash in the short term. This can be the biggest confusion for entrepreneurs, so let me explain. If you are selling fruit on a street corner for cash, buying it on the wholesale market and ditching unsold fruit at the end of the day, then the increase in cash in your pocket from what you have sold over and above what you paid for the fruit in the morning is both cash and profit. But as soon as you start selling on account, buying on account and keeping stock, then profit and cash are different in the short term, because there is a time lag between when you receive something and then pay for it, and between what you sell and then what you get paid for it.

Costs

There are two kinds of costs for accounting purposes: variable costs, for example the cost of the bread, mayo and anchovy in a sandwich, and fixed costs (overheads) such as rent and marketing. This distinction helps calculate break-even, a term I will explain below.

Why balance sheets balance

Balance sheets balance because of the dual entry principle (see definitions). To explain what I mean, it's worth thinking about the balance sheet that is created when you start the business. For accounting purposes, if you start up your business with £1,000 of investment this will create two entries in the balance sheet. On one side of the balance sheet you will see an entry under current assets for cash. On the other side of the balance sheet you will see an entry under shareholders' funds for £1,000 of share capital. As you add financial things to your company, e.g. the purchase of a van, the balance sheet will show the value of the new assets you buy and perhaps a liability for the loan you took out to buy the van, or alternatively a reduction in the cash balance because you have used cash to buy the van.

The profits or losses you make in the business, as well as being shown in the profit and loss account, will also be shown in the balance sheet. This dual method of reporting the numbers is known as double-entry bookkeeping.

While the profit and loss account and cash flows are records of what happens over a certain period of time, the balance sheet is always a record of the state of play in your business at a point in time.

While the balance sheet is therefore not terribly helpful day to day, it is an important record of where the business is on a certain date. As such, it is very useful for investors and particularly bankers, especially if you want to borrow money as it shows the assets and liabilities of the business – in particular, is it solvent, is it over-borrowed and officially does it have enough liquidity to meet its current bills, i.e. it shows the financial riskiness of the business.

Some common questions on preparing projections

What software do I need?

Nearly all projections are prepared using Excel in the first instance. Most investors like to be sent a copy of the projections in Excel (if you have used another software package you can usually export them to Excel) so they can "play" with your projection model. Sometimes they will refer to this as "stress testing".

What do you mean by "model"?

Investors want to see a financial model that integrates profit and loss projections, a cash flow projection and balance sheets. This will typically cover three to five years with at least years one and two prepared on a monthly basis.

How far have I got to project?

There are two schools of thought here – either three years or five years. Personally I like five years, even though investors often say that they pay no attention to anything beyond two years. I prefer five years because it's only after this length of time that a typical company will really start to motor and give you a true vision of where you want to get to and hence the future value of the business.

Preparing projections

Take the job of preparing your projections seriously. Typically it will take you between one and three days, depending on the amount of research you need to do before you start preparing the numbers.

Bear in mind that preparing projections is an iterative process, i.e. you will do the steps below and then keep going backwards and forwards as you tweak the numbers until you come up with something that feels right.

Before you start

First you should assemble the assumptions for the first draft of the numbers. It is a good idea to make sure you document your assumptions as you go along, as it will be useful for you but also very useful for investors when they come to look at the numbers. You can use the assumptions in the supporting text that will accompany your projections.

Another thing to bear in mind is that if your business is VAT registered, you should calculate the following figures excluding VAT (except for your personal budget).

- **Step 1:** Do a personal budget (sadly you do need to include VAT for this!). Before you start your business you need to know how much you need to live on. Investors don't want you couch surfing; they want you hammering away on the business.
- **Step 2:** Decide on your selling price. You may not think you need to do this until you have worked out your costs, but in fact you do! Your selling price determines your customer position. Ikea is famous for starting with the price in new product development. Obviously your price must at least cover all your costs. You may have to revisit your sales price after you have looked at your costs and you may have to go through this process several times before you come to the right numbers. (The iterative bit!)
- **Step 3:** Identify your distribution channels – how you reach your customers, for example through the internet or via a pop-up. You can then project the sales you think you will make through each of these channels.
- **Step 4:** Forecast volumes by main product category for each channel identified in Step 3. Think about the pipeline of "prospects" you need to reach and the conversion rate. This is the hardest step of all. If your projections are going to go wrong it will be on the sales line assumption. Don't underestimate how long it takes to build up sales. Go to trade shows, network and talk to related businesses to get an idea of a *realistic* rate of sales growth. For example, in fashion,

even if you don't sell shoes, find out how long it took LK Bennett to build up her business and, say, open her third shop. This will give you a benchmark for your own business.

- **Step 5:** Forecast your fixed (overhead) costs. Usually this is the easiest part of your forecast.
- **Step 6:** Work out your variable costs per product. If you are running a service business or an internet information type one, do not be surprised if you have a few variable costs.
- **Step 7:** Work out what equipment the business will need to buy and when.
- **Step 8:** Find out what the payment terms are for your industry, i.e. how long do you expect to have to wait to be paid and how long is normal for you to take to pay your bills. Work this into your projections, as it is often the late payers in your business that will stop you having the cash you need to pay bills today and grow tomorrow.
- **Step 9:** Think about what levels of stock you will need to maintain.

You now have all the information to plug into a model to create your projections. Before doing that you can now estimate what your break-even might look like.

To calculate your break-even

Break-even is where sales = total costs. It is the first major financial milestone as the business moves from loss to profit.

To calculate break-even if you have just one product or service follow the steps shown below.

- Take your selling price and deduct the variable costs per unit. This gives you the contribution per unit.
- Now take your fixed overheads and divide them by the contribution per unit.

The result is the break-even level of sales in units.

If you have more than one product at significantly different levels of profit per unit, then your break-even will depend on your mix of sales. So the calculation is more complicated.

You will need to make a table with products, selling prices, variable costs, contribution per product, and percentage of sales (which should add up to 100%!). If you multiply each contribution per product by the percentage of sales and add this up, this will give you your "weighted" average contribution per product sold.

Now divide overheads by this to get your break-even point and ask yourself if it looks reasonable and look at how long it will take you to get to break-even.

Don't be surprised if you find yourself going backwards and forwards several times in terms of pricing, variable costs and overhead assumptions before you get to a business model that looks and feels right and, importantly, means you have a product or products that lots of customers are actually likely to buy!

Putting your numbers in your business plan

So where do the numbers go in your business plan?

In the executive summary, include a small table showing year-by-year sales, gross profit (and margin, as a percentage) and net profit. You should also describe when you will break even and show a small table of your cash flow projections, with a special reference to when you will have the lowest amount of cash available.

It might also be worth including a short summary of the assumptions you have made to reach these numbers, e.g. the number of units you will sell each year.

In the chapter on finance you should have a summary profit and loss and cash flow and possibly a balance sheet, along with some narrative below each set of numbers explaining your assumptions.

In the appendix, you should include full financial projections, maybe with additional supporting data or assumptions. Usually, entrepreneurs print off the spreadsheets and add them to the business plan.

You can put all the extra information behind the numbers into the appendix. For example, you can add the detailed assumptions and extra information on what is likely to happen to the numbers if things go better or worse than expected, known as the sensitivity analysis. This shows you understand business risk. Indeed, although it is not usual, some entrepreneurs will include three different sets of numbers in the appendix: the base case (i.e. what you really expect to happen), the optimistic case (i.e. if things go better than expected) and the pessimistic case (i.e. if things go worse than expected).

Appendix V

Important legal things to know about crowd funding

By Gillian Roche-Saunders at Bovill Ltd (www.bovill.com)

Although it may sometimes seem this way, crowd funding is not being ignored by the authorities that regulate business, especially those interested in how financial investment takes place. As crowd funding has become more popular and more accessible to the general public, the authorities that regulate financial services have become increasingly interested. This increased interest has been global and in the UK, the FCA, as main regulator, and the government have been taking notice.

Now that some established platforms have opted to become regulated, you may be wondering whether and when to select a regulated platform. Your experience as a funder or fund seeker is likely to be different depending on which option you choose: regulated platforms will need to comply with many rules about the information they must provide and the checks that they must undertake on funders and fund seekers. These rules may offer you more protection but the cost of this is likely to be a slower sign-up process.

When weighing up your options, the questions below may help you to assess what you will gain and lose depending on the route you pick and to think about what else you want to be aware of from a regulatory point of view.

Details of whether a particular crowd funding platform is authorised and what permission they have been given by the FCA can be found on the FCA website: www.fsa.gov.uk/register/firmSearchForm.do.

General questions

Should the funding platform or intermediary be regulated?

The answer to this depends on what type of crowd funding you are dealing with.

- **Donations:** A platform that arranges for donations to be made, with no expectation of a reward, repayment or other interest, does not need to be regulated.
- **Pledges:** Pledges that are non-financial can be arranged by an unregulated platform. However, if the reward is financial, regulation may be required. This is especially likely to be the case if the financial reward is the main reason for investing.
- **Equity:** If the platform arranges for investors to purchase shares in companies, the platform will need to be regulated by the FCA unless an exemption applies.
- **Lending:** There was not always a clear-cut answer to this simple question but, from 2014, lending platforms need to be regulated by the FCA unless an exemption applies.

Am I the client?

Some platforms offer their services to the funder, others to the fund seeker, and depending on this you may or may not be their client. If you are the client of a regulated platform you are owed extra obligations, such as the platform acting in your best interests and providing you with additional information. Check your agreement with the platform to find out more.

Who holds my money?

In some models funders are asked to deposit funds into an account before it is needed by the fund seeker. In other cases funds due to fund seekers may be held for a time before they are drawn down. This money needs to be kept safe while it is not in your hands. You should also check that it is kept in a segregated client account that contains only client money and has been granted trust status. If this is a UK bank, you may also have Financial Services Compensation Scheme protection (see below).

Will I receive fair treatment?

You may want to know what the platform's policy is on treating funders and fund seekers fairly. Regulated firms must act in the best interests of their clients and there may be a summary of these in your agreement with the platform.

Am I protected?

It is good to know what level of protection is available to you. The platform may have controls in place to limit the possibility of the other person failing to keep up their side of their funding contract – check the website and your agreement for further details on how protected you are.

Equally, when you use a regulated firm as your platform, adviser or custodian, you may have some protection under the useful schemes set out below. This is more likely to be the case if you are the client (see above). To find out more about the protections in place, check your agreement with the platform.

- The Financial Ombudsman Service can consider complaints about the service provided by regulated firms: check if your funding platform comes under their jurisdiction.
- The Financial Services Compensation Scheme can provide cover for any claims made against regulated firms that have defaulted. This may be particularly relevant if you have to hand over money ahead of the funding target being reached.

Funder questions

Who holds my investment?

Keeping investments safe is a crucial task and regulated firms often offer this service either directly, using a nominee company or using another firm entirely (often referred to as the custodian). If a regulated firm looks after your investment, whether that is a share, a unit or a form of loan note, it is likely that they need permission to "safeguard and administer assets".

Is my funding being put to legitimate use?

The platform should tell you what level of due diligence they undertake on the fund seeker. Regulated platforms must undertake certain due diligence steps on investee companies to ensure that there is no financial crime occurring. If a regulated platform is also managing your investment, it is likely to go to extra lengths to make sure that the investments they make on your behalf are sound.

Have I been fully informed of the risks?

The risks of funding should be explained to you by the platform. Regulated platforms will have to set out all the risks for you in easy-to-understand language so that you can make sensible choices about whether the funding arrangement is right for you. Issues such as diversification, difficulty in selling your shares, ensuring loan repayments or receiving your reward should be made clear to you; if you did not receive enough advice or have any follow-up questions, make sure you ask the platform or a financial adviser before funding.

Fund seeker questions

Are the funds I receive legitimate?

The platform should tell you what level of due diligence they undertake on funders. Regulated platforms must undertake certain due diligence steps on investors to ensure that there is no financial crime occurring. If you are seeking equity investment, this may be particularly important as the investors will have an ongoing relationship with you as your shareholders.

Is my marketing material compliant?

When you promote investments, there are a number of rules and regulations you need to be aware of. This will particularly be the case for equity investments but may also apply to loan-based and financial reward-based funding.

- If you want your marketing material to be available to the general public and your company is not a regulated firm, your promotions will need to be approved by an FCA-authorised firm and the contents may need to be adjusted in order for them to do so.
- If you are happy to limit your audience to certain types of individuals, such as high net worth individuals, you may be able to market without the approval referred to above. To do so you will need to comply with the requirements of the FSMA 2000 (Financial Promotion) Order 2001. These rules differ depending on your target audience and so you will need to identify who you are likely to market to.
- If your funding target is over €5m, you may need to issue a prospectus under the Prospectus Directive.
- If you are a private company, you should consider whether you can offer shares to the public in light of the restriction in Companies Act 2006 s755.

Appendix VI

The Enterprise Investment Scheme and the Seed Enterprise Investment Scheme

By Mark Stemp, tax director at Crowe Clark Whitehill (www.croweclarkwhitehill.co.uk)

The government provides numerous tax incentives to encourage investment in small trading companies, the most relevant schemes for crowd funding being the Enterprise Investment Scheme (EIS) and the Seed Enterprise Investment Scheme (SEIS). As with all tax reliefs, there are numerous qualifying conditions. This appendix covers the main features of the two schemes as a guide only; detailed tax advice should be sought prior to investment.

The Enterprise Investment Scheme

The EIS was introduced in 1994 to help small, unquoted companies raise finance to grow their businesses. The scheme allows investors who subscribe for ordinary shares in certain small companies to claim tax reliefs.

Most UK trading businesses qualify, the main exceptions being those involved in property development, property rental, operating a hotel, accountancy and legal services. Other conditions to be met by the company are as follows:

- less than £15m of gross assets prior to the share issue and no more than £16m after
- must have fewer than 250 employees
- must be unquoted and have no arrangements in place to become quoted (for these purposes, companies listed on the AIM and PLUS markets are unquoted)
- can raise up to £5m under the scheme in any rolling 12-month period
- must spend the money raised on the trade within two years.

Where the company issuing the shares is the parent company of a trading group, the above limits apply to the group as a whole.

HMRC operates an advance assurance service that allows the fundraising company to obtain written confirmation that the company qualifies for the scheme. It is common to share this confirmation with potential investors.

Investors cannot be connected with the company for a period before and after the issue. The connected rules are complex but the main rule means that the investor along with close family or business partners, cannot own more than 30% of the share capital in the company. They also cannot be an employee of the company. Investors can become a paid director after investing, provided the remuneration payable is reasonable. Where investors receive other value from the company, such as use of company assets, the value of the benefit should be insignificant in relation to the amount subscribed for shares to prevent a claw back of relief.

The reliefs available to qualifying investors are detailed below.

Income tax relief

An investor can claim 30% income tax relief on the amount that they invest in qualifying EIS shares. This means that for an investment of £50,000, £15,000 of income tax relief can be claimed, reducing the net cost of investment to £35,000.

Relief is available in the tax year the shares are issued or can be carried back to the preceding tax year. Relief is capped at the lower of that year's maximum investment limit (in 2012–13, the limit for an investor was £1m) and the tax liability of the investor in the year the relief is to be claimed (bearing in mind that the tax credit on dividends is non-refundable).

The shares must be held for three years to retain the income tax relief, otherwise the relief is clawed back.

Capital gains tax deferral

Where an EIS investor has realised a gain on the disposal of any asset within the period of three years before the date of issue of the shares until 12 months after the date of issue of the shares, it is possible for the capital gains tax (CGT) payable on that gain to be deferred.

The EIS subscription can be set off against the gain realised. The gain then becomes taxable to CGT in the year in which the EIS shares are sold, subject to the availability of capital losses at that time. However, investors should take note that the tax rate could have increased (or more hopefully decreased) in that later year.

There is no investment limit on the amount that qualifies for this relief.

It is possible to claim both of the above tax reliefs on an investment. The effect of this is to reduce the initial cost to 42% of the initial investment.

Capital gains tax exemption

When an investor sells their EIS shares, any gain on the shares will be exempt from CGT provided that there has been no claw back of the income tax relief.

For example, if an investor invests £50,000 into shares and subsequently sells for £75,000, there would normally be a chargeable gain of £25,000 subject to CGT at up to 28%, a tax bill of up to £7,000. If the shares were EIS qualifying shares, the gain would be exempt from tax.

In addition to the EIS reliefs, qualifying investments may also qualify for other tax reliefs, including inheritance tax relief and loss relief.

Inheritance tax relief

Once the shares are held for two years, and provided there has been no claw back of income tax relief, they will qualify for 100% relief from inheritance tax. This means that, if an investor dies and has owned the shares for a minimum of two years, there will be no inheritance tax to pay on their value. The full rate of inheritance tax is currently 40%.

Loss relief

In the unfortunate circumstance that the shares are sold at a loss or the company goes into liquidation, relief is available against either capital gains or income. For an investor claiming relief against income at 40%, relief of 58% of the initial investment is available.

Let's look at an example where an investor purchased £50,000 of shares and four years later the shares became worthless.

Investment into shares	£50,000	100%
EIS income tax relief @ 30%	£15,000	30%
Net cost of investment	£35,000	
Loss of the net cost – to set off against income	£35,000	
Income tax relief (40% taxpayer)	£14,000	28%
Loss on the investment after all reliefs	£21,000	42%

The investor in this case has invested £50,000, received tax relief totalling £29,000, and so has lost £21,000.

The reliefs alter the risk/reward ratio, reducing the downside risk to an investor by protecting an element of the capital by way of tax relief. It also enhances any returns if the business is successful.

Claiming income tax and capital gains tax deferral relief

An investor can claim relief once they have received the relevant tax certificate issued by the company (form EIS 3). The administrative process is as follows.

- The company needs to complete and submit form EIS 1 to HMRC. This can only be done once the business has been trading for four months. This is not a problem for a company already trading, but can delay the process if the business is just starting.
- HMRC will examine the information submitted and if they are content that the company qualifies, they will issue the company with form EIS 2 authorising the company to issue tax certificates.
- The company will issue forms EIS 3 to the investors.

There are many different ways in which investors can claim the tax reliefs. Most frequently, it is done by submitting the completed form EIS 3 certificate to HMRC to have the relief included in their PAYE code or alternatively by making a claim on their self-assessment tax return.

The Seed Enterprise Investment Scheme

The SEIS was introduced for shares issued between 6th April 2012 and 5th April 2017. This scheme, which operates in a similar way to EIS, offers enhanced tax reliefs for investors in early stage and small companies.

The specific qualifying conditions for companies wishing to raise funds under SEIS are as follows:

- assets of less than £200,000 immediately prior to the share issue
- fewer than 50 employees
- the trade being funded by the share issue must be less than two years old

- a cumulative limit of £150,000 only can be raised by a company under SEIS. Once this limit is reached, fundraising can continue using EIS.

Investors can invest up to £100,000 per year into SEIS qualifying shares. The tax reliefs for investors are:

- 50% income tax relief on the amount subscribed (relief is capped at the investor's tax liability and can be claimed in the year of investment or in the preceding year; however, it should be noted that 2012–13 is the first year relief is available so no "carry back" is allowed)
- exemption from CGT on the sale of the shares
- a CGT "holiday" where gains realised in 2012–13 are reinvested into a SEIS. Such gains will be exempt from CGT. It is expected that investments made in 2013–14 can be carried back to 2012–13 and still benefit from this relief.

The shares need to be retained for three years to prevent claw back of the reliefs. Should all reliefs be available to an investor, they should be able to recover 78% of their initial investment. The inheritance tax and loss reliefs should also apply as set out for EIS above. For SEIS shares acquired in 2012–13 where all of the above reliefs have been claimed, a future loss on the disposal of the shares can result in total tax relief of 100.5% of the investment cost.

Let's look at an example where an investor purchased £50,000 of shares and four years later the shares became worthless.

Investment into shares	£50,000	100%
SEIS income tax relief @ 50%	£25,000	50%
Net cost of investment	£25,000	
Loss of the net cost – to set off against income	£25,000	
Income tax relief (45% taxpayer)	£11,250	22.5%
Loss on the investment after all reliefs	£13,750	42%
Loss on the investment after all reliefs	£13,750	
Already claimed relief of CGT holiday on reinvestment	£14,000	28%
Net profit after all reliefs	£250	

The investor in this case has invested £50,000 but claimed tax relief of £50,250, a profit of £250 despite losing their investment value entirely.

Summary

Both EIS and SEIS should be considered an attractive way to encourage investment by reducing the capital investors have at risk within the business as well as ensuring a tax-free gain on disposal.

Appendix VII

Further reading, useful websites and people to follow in the crowd

Books

New books are being published all the time, but here are some that are particularly relevant.

- *The Kickstarter Handbook: Real-life success stories of artists, inventors, and entrepreneurs* by Don Steinberg, Quirk Books
- *The Crowdfunding Bible: How to raise money for any startup, video game or project* by Scott Steinberg and Rusel DeMaria, Read.me
- *The Crowdfunding Revolution: How to raise venture capital using social media* by Kevin Lawton and Dan Marom, McGraw Hill
- *The Kickstarter Handbook: Real-life crowdfunding success stories* by Don Steinberg, Quirk Books
- *The Secrets of Crowdfunding* by Sean Akers, Sean Akers
- *Crowdfund It!* by Anne Maguire, Editia
- *The Crowdfunding Bible: How to raise money for any startup,*

video game or project by Scott Steinberg and Rusel DeMaria, Read.me
- *The Everything Guide to Crowdfunding* by Thomas Elliott Young, Adams Media
- *CrowdFunding 2.0: The 7 dumbest mistakes when raising finance for your company* by Simon Dixon, Bank to the Future

Useful websites

There is loads of useful information on the web about crowd funding. Here is a selection of websites to start you off.

- UK Crowdfunding Association: www.ukcfa.org.uk
- P2P Finance Association: www.p2pfinanceassociation.org.uk
- National Crowdfunding Association: www.nlcfa.org/main. html (US)
- National Crowdfunding Association of Canada: www. ncfacanada.org (Canada)
- European Crowdfunding Association: http://crowdfunding.is (EU)
- Crowdfunding News: http://crowdfundingnews.co.uk (UK) – includes a directory of crowd funding platforms
- Crowdsourcing.org: www.crowdsourcing.org
- Crowd Funding Forum: http://crowdfundingforum.com/ forum.php?s=7a8045d84c651a8ebdf53b34c28addfa
- Crowdfunding Code: www.crowdfundingcode.com – selling crowd funding lessons – please note this is for information only; we do not recommend the lessons or other content
- Crowdfund Capital Advisors: www.crowdfundcapitaladvisors. com
- Crowd Valley: www.crowdvalley.com

Other online resources

LinkedIn and Facebook groups

LinkedIn

- Crowdsourcing and Crowdfunding: www.linkedin.com/groups ?gid=3185331&mostPopular=&trk=tyah
- Crowdfunding: www.linkedin.com/groups?gid=1985057&most Popular=&trk=tyah
- Crowdsourcing and Crowdfunding (members only): www. linkedin.com/groups?home=&gid=3713252&trk=anet_ug_hm
- Crowdsourcing Analytics: www.linkedin.com/groups/ CrowdSourcing-Analytics-3838486?gid=3838486&mostPopular =&trk=tyah

Facebook

- AppsFunder: www.facebook.com/AppsFunder
- CrowdFunding-Website-Reviews.com: www.facebook.com/ BestCrowdfundingWebsiteReviews
- Sportfunder: www.facebook.com/SportFunder
- Silicon Crowdfunding: www.facebook.com/ SiliconCrowdfunding
- Crowd Funding Film: www.facebook.com/pages/Crowd-funding-film/130364697011861

Blogs

It is also worth checking on blogs for crowd funding news, especially:

- www.crowdfundingblogs.com
- http://crowdfundingsitesblog.com
- www.thecrowdfundingrevolution.com
- blog.rockethub.com
- blog.indiegogo.com

Twitter

Here are some people who comment on crowd funding. You can also search for news using the hash tag #crowdfunding.

Commentator
Modwenna Rees-Mogg @modwenna

Pledge
Perry Chen/Kickstarter @perrychen
IndieGoGo @indiegogo

Equity
Darren Westlake/Crowdcube @crowdcube
Jeff Lynn/Seedrs @Jeffseedrs
Simon Dixon/Bank to the Future @simondixontwitt
Syndicate Room @syndicate_room

Alternative debt
Anil Stocker/MarketInvoice @anilstocker
Platform Black @platformblack

Debt
James Meeking/Funding Circle @fundingcircle
Graeme Marshall/Funding Knight @fundingknight
Giles Andrews/Zopa @zopagiles
Kevin Caley/ThinCats @thincatsuk

Social enterprise
Kiva @kiva
Buzzbnk @buzzbnk

Alternative and other areas
Abundance Generation @Abundancegen
Crowdbnk @crowdbnk

Appendix VIII

Other places to find funding

A quick summary

Debt funding

If you are looking for debt funding, it is still well worth approaching all the banks on the high street, not just your own. Many governments have put in place incentives to the banks to lend to smaller businesses, and if you approach a bank in the right way you might just find that they are willing to lend to you. Remember that in talking to them you will learn how crowd debt funders might think too!

A small number of venture capitalists, known as venture debt providers, also lend companies money, but remember that they lend on very aggressive terms.

For young entrepreneurs, the UK government is providing small start-up loans under the Start-Up Loans scheme. There's more information at www.greatbusiness.gov.uk/start-up-loans.

Angel funding

The best starting points for finding out about angel funding are AngelNews (www.angelnews.co.uk) and the UK Business Angels Association (www.ukbusinessangelsassociation.org.uk).

If you are based outside the UK, search for your local business angel trade association. If you are in the EU, the European Trade Association for Business Angels (www.eban.org) is a very useful starting point.

Venture capital funding

The best way to research venture capital funding in the UK is to start with the British Private Equity and Venture Capital Association (www.bvca.co.uk), or find your national venture capital association if you are in another country.

But the best way to raise venture capital funding is to find yourself an excellent (not a rubbish one – do your research!) corporate finance adviser and hire him or her to help you conduct your fundraising.

Your friends and family

Don't be afraid to ask your friends and family for backing, but be ready to be rejected and don't let rejection destroy your relationship. If they do back you, make sure that you get everything properly written down from a legal perspective to avoid heartache in the future.

Acknowledgements

No book is ever done on your own and this one is no exception. As always, Crimson Publishing has given me an encouraging and supportive team to support me, but I would like to thank first and foremost Jenny McLaren for her invaluable assistance in helping me write this book. Without her it simply would not have happened, nor would it have been half as good as it is. Jenny, your attention to detail and ability to grasp what is needed are stunning.

Many thanks also to the other contributors to this book, including Johnny Martin, the teams at Bovill, Crowe Clark Whitehill and Gill Jennings & Every, who provided vital financial, legal, tax and IP expertise. I am also very grateful to the hundreds of people in the crowd – from investors to entrepreneurs and platform operators – who gave so much and made the subject so much clearer, and gave me a deeper knowledge of all the different aspects of the subject matter. I hope you enjoy your copies when you receive them.

Lastly, I would like to recognise the indirect contribution of the team at AngelNews and Pitching for Management, who kept the work fires burning while I researched and wrote the book. Thanks Sarah, Fuchsia, Sandra, Caroline, Hatty and Debbie! And, of course, I could not have done it without the support of my family, who allowed me to take such valuable family time to work on it.

William Rees-Mogg
July 1928 – December 2012
RIP